The T&G Story

D1380750

The T&G Story

A History of the Transport and General Workers Union 1922–2007

Andrew Murray

London
Lawrence & Wishart 2008

Lawrence and Wishart Limited
99a Wallis Road
London
E9 5LN

Published in association with the T&G Section of Unite the Union
First published 2008

British Library Cataloguing in Publication Data.

A catalogue record for this book is available from the British Library

ISBN 9781905007745 837

Text setting Etype, Liverpool
Printed and bound by Cambridge University Press

Contents

Introduction   7

Acknowledgements   11

1 Formation and emergence 1889-1922   13

2 General strike and depression 1923-1939   48

3 The T&G at war 1939-1945   77

4 Cold war trade unionism 1945-1956   93

5 A progressive union 1956-1969   114

6 The world the T&G made 1969-1979   139

7 The T&G world unmade 1979-2003   171

8 Into Unite 2003-2007   198

9 In place of a conclusion   215

Bibliography   217

Index   219

Introduction

The Transport and General Workers Union holds a central place in the history of twentieth-century Britain and Ireland. It was the largest, most representative and important working-class organisation in Britain for much of the century, and its influence – both direct and indirect – extended beyond industry to help shape the broad social development of the country.

Into its ranks were organised millions of working men and women, of almost every trade and in every corner of the country. From those ranks came some of the most remarkable leaders of the labour movement, and indeed society more generally. The names of Ernest Bevin, Frank Cousins and Jack Jones must feature prominently in any serious general history of twentieth century Britain.

It is impossible to gauge accurately the number of people who passed through the union, but it certainly runs to many millions. At its peak, at the end of the 1970s, the T&G had over 2,100,000 members and was turning over in excess of 250,000 members a year (although records were not necessarily entirely accurate). A vast proportion of the working people of Britain have held a T&G card at some time or other in their working lives.

For many, of course, holding a card would have been all that they did. For a majority, the meaning of the union was restricted to the role it played in their own workplace, no more and no less. But for tens of thousands it was the main vehicle for their engagement in the wider society – as members of committees or delegates to external organisations, and as representatives and officials; sometimes it was the first step towards becoming a councillor or an MP.

And the number of people whose lives have been changed as a result of T&G activity is much larger even than its membership. The union was connected to broader political activity through its organisation in the wider labour movement and its affiliation to the Labour Party. These alliances have been the engine of profound social transformation, the consequences of which have been felt across the country in the massive improvements of conditions in workplaces and working-class communities.

In the historic weight given to great trade unions, some might see the T&G taking second place to the National Union of Mineworkers (and its predecessor the MFGB). The NUM, however, did not and could not have a similar reach throughout society as a whole – it was (and is) a single-industry union, almost entirely male and white, and based in communities which were often physically isolated from the rest of the working class. The T&G, in contrast, was rooted everywhere, spreading from its origins primarily in the docks to cover almost every industry and form of employment; and it could be found in every town. Its membership was a very fair representation of the working-class as a whole – indeed those members elected Britain's first black trade union leader, and then elected a woman to serve as his deputy at the end of the millennium.

For most of its 85-year history, the union was the biggest single influence within the TUC and the largest trade union affiliate to the Labour Party. As Party Leader, Neil Kinnock once famously declared that in many ways 'the T&G *is* the Labour Party'. This was a controversial claim, but it was not a foolish one, nor one that could conceivably have been made about any other organisation.

The story of the T&G is now ripe for telling because it has an ending, with the decision of the union's members to merge with Amicus and thereby create Unite, a new trade union for the twenty-first century. Whatever may befall its culture and traditions, the name of the Transport and General Workers Union is now passing into history.

It is, in fact, surprising that there exists no previous single-volume general history of the union. Indeed, the historiography of the T&G is very sketchy and full of gaps. There are, of course, two magnificent biographies of T&G general secretaries, which, for the period of activity of their subjects, almost constitute union histories. These are Alan Bullock's *The Life and Times of Ernest Bevin* (the first of the three volumes is most relevant to the T&G story) and Geoffrey Goodman's life of Frank Cousins, *Awkward Warrior*. There is no biography of Jack Jones, the third in the trinity of great T&G leaders, though his memoirs, published as *Union Man*, go some way towards filling that particular hole. V.L. Allen's *Trade Union Leadership* is in part a description of the workings of the T&G in the post-World War Two period, and in part a biography of its then leader Arthur Deakin. I have drawn heavily on all of these works in the corresponding chapters of this book.

Beyond these books there are a number of general histories of British trade unionism, which cannot but dwell extensively on the T&G; in particular the volumes by Allen Hutt and Francis Williams must be mentioned here, though they write from differing political points of view. Then there are a number of memoirs by T&G activists, and a smaller number of studies of particular parts of the union, among which Ken Fuller's work on the London Bus section is of exceptional value.

The only previous attempt to write a comprehensive history of the union was embarked upon by Ken Coates and the late Tony Topham. Alas, their monumental first volume, covering the union's development and emergence, only brought the story up to 1922, the year the union was formed. This is unlikely ever to be bettered in terms of the scope of its treatment of the subject matter, but, self-evidently, it does not constitute a history of the T&G.

The present work does not aspire to match the erudition of Coates and Topham. My aim has been to reduce the T&G story to manageable dimensions, in order that it may be read by the interested activist, and reach beyond the academic market. That is not such an easy task, since the T&G's history leads off in any number of directions – little in British economic, political and social development has not been touched by it. Thus, to take the histories of the 'great men' referred to above, the story of Bevin is also the story of wartime government and the formation of NATO; the story of Cousins is also that of the Wilson government; and that of Jones also the story of the Spanish Civil War.

These byways cannot be explored in this book beyond the minimum requirements imposed by context; and there are many other significant aspects of the union's life that are not touched upon here more than in passing. There is certainly a book to be written on the role of women in the T&G, a book about the development of the shop stewards movement, a book about trade unionism in aviation and so on. There should be a biography of Bill Morris too. I am also particularly conscious that the story of the T&G in Ireland does not have the treatment here that it deserves, united with and separate from the story of the union in Britain as it is. All those are works for the future, and important ones.

Acknowledgements

As far as this volume is concerned, I have benefited from considerable assistance. Pride of place must go to Geoffrey Goodman, who knows more about the history of the T&G than anyone alive. He has been unstinting in his expert advice, and I have also of course used his written works on the subject, his biography of Cousins above all. Geoffrey has been collaborating with me on a DVD to appear in parallel with this book, and I have quoted freely from a number of interviews he conducted for that purpose. Thanks too to our other collaborators on the film, Jack Amos and Rob Wright of Red Flag Productions. The fruits of their researches are reflected here, and Jack did the interviews with Mick Connolly and Brenda Sanders.

I have also been helped by a number of colleagues at the T&G, above all Ray Collins, the assistant general secretary for administration, who has lived this history for the last thirty-six years and understands it better than most. He has a most interesting memoir in him should he ever choose to write it, but for the time being he has limited himself to some useful observations on this text. In places I have drawn on work done by veteran T&G journalist Mike Pentelow for the *T&G Record*. Graham Stevenson also read the manuscript and made a number of useful comments. And thanks of course to Sally Davison at Lawrence and Wishart for her support for this project.

With such assistance it is particularly important to underline that the opinions and perspective on the T&G's history here are all mine. This book is supported by the union, of which I have been an employee for most of the last twenty-one years, but it is not an 'official' history. Where there have been controversies within the union (which is to say more or less continually) I have endeavoured to outline both 'sides', but judgments have to be made and, right or wrong, they are my responsibility alone.

This book is published in the hope that present and future generations of trade unionists may profit from a study of the struggles of the T&G membership to create a better world, from their workplaces outwards. Those struggles have played a large part in shaping the world we live in today. As such the T&G story is bound to be controversial. My own view on it is the same as that of Ken Coates: 'People should be very proud of the traditions of this trade union. It is really the uncelebrated story of everything that is good in Britain'.[1]

Andrew Murray, London, April 2008

Notes

1. Coates/Topham (2), p18.

Photo acknowledgements

All pictures in the text are courtesy of the T&G, except as follows:

Page 183, Margaret Prosser, © Joanne O'Brien
Page 201, Tony Woodley, © Simon Clark/Insight
Page 204, House of Commons cleaners, © Joanne O'Brien
Page 207, Gate Gourmet, © Joanne O'Brien
Page 208, London Buses, © Mark Thomas
Page 213, Voting for merger, © Roy Peters
Page 213, Honouring the past, © Rod Leon

1. Formation and emergence 1889–1922

The Transport and General Workers Union was born in 1922, its immediate emergence shaped above all by the turbulent industrial struggles that followed the First World War. Its roots, however, go far deeper into the past of the labour movement in Britain and Ireland. Indeed, they can be traced back to the iconic pioneers of English trade unionism, the Tolpuddle Martyrs, since the union these men ultimately created – the National Union of Agricultural Workers – merged into the T&G in 1982. And the T&G also came to include the National Union of Vehicle Builders, formed by Lancashire coachmakers in 1834, and the National Association of Operative Plasterers, set up by London building workers at around the same time.

THE RETURNED 'CONVICTS'

| James Brine | Thomas Stanfield | John Stanfield | George Loveless | James Loveless |
| Aged 25 | Aged 51 | Aged 25 | Aged 41 | Aged 29 |

The Tolpuddle Martyrs

But that would perhaps be to run ahead of the story. The T&G as founded in 1922 was overwhelmingly a transport workers' union, and primarily a dockers' one: it was the existing unions for dockworkers that took the lead in the great amalgamation. It therefore makes sense to begin the history of the T&G with the development of union organisation in the docks of its maritime homeland, and in particular with the great London Docks Strike of 1889.

Victorian trade unionism

The London Docks Strike was not just a landmark in the story of the unions that later formed the T&G; it was significant in the whole emergence of general trade unionism as a powerful social force in the land. Until the late nineteenth century, trade unionism had largely been the preserve of craft and skilled workers, and had tended to take the form of 'friendly societies', oriented towards insuring members against the vicissitudes of Victorian industrial life, rather than becoming the instruments of working-class struggle. A self-conscious effort to secure respectability for better off sections of workers was the governing characteristic of mid-Victorian trade unionism, rather than any attempt to organise the great impoverished mass of labour. (This was also the case in the early years of the TUC itself – founded in 1868.)

The historians Morton and Tate described the situation: 'The old craft unions ... became mere sick and burial clubs: they would not support strikes even against wage cuts or increased hours. The old leaders, often saturated with the economic and political ideas of the capitalists, were largely devoid of any positive policy whereby their organisations could grow and assert their power in the way which the times so urgently demanded.'[1]

Yet the social conditions prevailing cried out for militant industrial and political struggle to secure change. Beyond a very small number of highly skilled workers, the working class of the 1870s and 1880s faced a life of deprivation and insecurity outside the workplace, and a regime without rights, protection or redress within it. The rapid economic progress of Britain in the nineteenth century rested above all on the ruthless exploitation of labour under the application of *laissez-faire* principles. These were supported by both the Tory and Liberal parties, who ruled from a parliament that was elected through a process that excluded many working-class men and all women.

And there was no greater concentration of suffering in Britain than in the East End of London, the very heart of Britain's trading and commercial empire. Through here passed much of the vast trade generated by Britain's industrial supremacy, colonial possessions and growing economy. It was, in the words of Marx's collaborator Frederick Engels, an 'immense haunt of misery', sunk in 'torpid despair'. Tens of thousands of workers, drawn from all parts of Britain and, on a very large scale, from Ireland, were herded together into overcrowded slum housing with poor or non-existent sanitation and a general absence of municipal services. Diet was appalling, health care absent and life expectancy correspondingly short. At the time of the Docks Strike the reforms of the late Victorian era still lay ahead.

'The East End of London is the hell of poverty. Like an enormous black, motionless, giant kraken, the poverty of London lies there in lurking silence and encircles with mighty tentacles the life and wealth of the City and of the West End,' wrote John Henry Mackay. Only around ten per cent of the population in East End constituencies had the right to vote.[2]

But the dockers were not the first to rebel against the prevailing conditions in the East End. They were preceded as pioneers of general trade unionism by the famous Match Girls, employed at Bryant and May's factory in Bow. The socialist agitator Annie Besant inspired a largely successful strike against the disgusting conditions in which the mostly young women had to work, and the accompanying employer tyranny. Many of these women had family connections with dockers. And Will Thorne led a gas workers' strike in East London a year later. From these conflicts emerged the trade union that became the General and Municipal Workers Union (today known as the GMB), and the foundations of general unionism.

However, these great struggles were overshadowed by the conflict in the docks in 1889. The huge workforce there teetered permanently on the edge of utter destitution and acute hunger, if not outright starvation. One cause of this was casualisation, a system under

Match Girls on strike

which dockers were hired to unload vessels for a day, a half-day or even an hour, with absolutely no guarantee of employment. At its most degraded this system required dockers to literally fight each other in order to gain the favour of a foreman and the possibility of a brief period of badly paid work. The dock employers had no obligations whatsoever towards this vast and hyper-exploited workforce, and the public authorities had little more.

One does not need to turn to a philanthropic reformer, still less an avowed socialist, to get a sense of the conditions of life of the London dockers. The testimony of the General Manager of the Millwall Docks, Colonel Birt, in 1888 will do:

> The poor fellows are miserably clad, scarcely with a boot on their foot, in a most miserable state; and they cannot run, their boots would not permit them ... There are men who come without having a bit of food in their stomachs perhaps since the previous day; they have worked for an hour and earned fivepence; their hunger will not allow them to continue; they take the fivepence in order that they may get food, perhaps the first food they have had for twenty-four hours ... these poor men have come on work without a farthing in their pockets; they have not anything to eat in the middle of the day ... by four o'clock their strength is utterly gone.[3]

'These were the men', Francis Williams observes, 'the leaders of the old trade unionism regarded as unworthy of attention. They were, they considered, completely unorganisable.'

The 1889 docks strike

Three men, above all others, took a different view – Ben Tillett, Tom Mann and John Burns. Tillett, thirty years old in 1889 and with a career as a circus-boy, a sailor and a shoemaker already behind him, had long been trying, with little conspicuous success, to establish trade unionism in docklands. He was to become the main organiser of the strike. Mann and Burns were both, by background, skilled engineers, so we can see at the birth of the T&G an outline of the alliance that was later to be reforged – first by Jack Jones and Hugh Scanlon in the 1970s, and ultimately by Tony Woodley and Derek Simpson in the twenty-first century, with the merger of their unions into Unite. Burns and Mann were also experienced socialist agitators, and played a central part in mobilising and maintaining broad support for the dockers.

The strike was sparked by a local conflict at the South West India Dock, but was soon spread under Tillett's leadership to cover the whole riverfront. The central demand was for a wage rate of six pence an hour (as opposed to the prevailing rate of four or five pence), and the equal division of bonuses. The strike became famous as the 'dockers' tanner' dispute. Over 30,000 dockers, with as many other workers again, took part in the five-week dispute which, after mediation by the Roman Catholic Cardinal Manning, resulted in an almost complete victory for the strikers.

Coal heavers during the 1889 London dock strike

One notable feature of the strike was that, for the first time, the union side made a deliberate effort to shape general public opinion and win it over to the side of the workers. This was accomplished with some success, and had a real effect on both the course of the dispute and its eventual outcome. As Sydney and Beatrice Webb, Fabian historians of early British trade unionism, put it (with a touch of their characteristic snobbery):

> An electric spark of sympathy with the poor dockers fired the enthusiasm of all classes of the community. Public disapproval hindered the dock companies from obtaining, even for their unskilled labour, sufficient blacklegs to take the strikers' place. A public subscription of £48,736 allowed Mr Burns to organise an elaborate system of strike pay, which not only maintained the honest docker, but also bribed every East End loafer to withhold his labour.[4]

Francis Williams noted the same point in his own comprehensive history of the movement, written fifty years after the Webbs:

> The dockers had no resources, private or public, to fall back on – the old well-tried weapon of starvation, victor in so many industrial battles, seemed certain to give the employers a quick and easy victory ... But the match girls had shown the way. The three organisers turned to the weapon of publicity. Day by day great processions of dockers with banners flying and bands playing paraded through the streets of London to Tower Hill where Burns and Tillett, both magnificent mass orators, moved all who listened with their presentation of the dockers' case. These processions provided a spectacle such as London had never previously known.[5]

Another aspect of the strike that has echoes in all the subsequent history of the T&G was the close connection, for the first time, of socialism with trade unionism. Tillett, Mann and

Burns were all socialists and members of the Social Democratic Federation at the time. The SDF was the first explicitly Marxist party to be formed in Britain, albeit one too dogmatic to play the full role in the movement which the times required. Much of this was the fault of its eccentric middle-class leader, H.M. Hyndman, who condemned the agreement that ended the docks strike (in particular the requirement of strikers to work alongside those who had scabbed during the dispute) and the conduct of the dockers' leaders. (This denunciation set another pattern that has since become familiar.) Hyndman's view was that: 'our comrades who are devoting so much time and energy to the formation of these unions of unskilled labour must never lose sight of the fact that the complete emancipation of labour from the thralldom of capital is the end to work for. This end can never be achieved by mere trade unionism'.[6]

Finally, one must note the worldwide support that the strike attracted – considerable sums of money were received from abroad, above all from Australian trade unionists. The vast antipodean assistance helped tip the balance towards victory. Thus began another T&G tradition – that of international working-class solidarity.

The significance of the great Dock Strike was summed up by Frederick Engels:

> It is the movement of the greatest promise we have had for years and I am proud and glad to have lived to see it. If Marx had lived to witness this! If these poor downtrodden men ... these odds and ends of all trades, fighting every morning at the dock gates for an engagement, if *they* can combine, and terrify by their resolution the mighty Dock Companies, truly then we need not despair of any section of the working class. This is the beginning of real life in the East End, and if successful will transform the whole character of the East End ... If the dockers get organised, all other sections will follow ... It is a glorious movement and again I envy those that can share in this work.[7]

Ben Tillet in conversation

The expansion of general unionism

Trade unionism was indeed irreversibly altered as a result of the docks strike and the preceding struggles in the East End. The immediate consequence was the formation of a large number of trade unions organising among unskilled labourers. In 1890 alone more than 200,000 workers were recruited to these unions, and overall trade union membership in the country doubled. To quote Francis Williams once more: 'not only had a great battle been fought and won and the dockers given a status they had never before possessed, the course of trade union history had itself been changed.' [8]

Tillett transformed his union into the Dock, Wharf, Riverside and General Labourers Union, which organised in nearly all the principal ports. Another union, the National Union of Dock Labourers, covered Liverpool, Glasgow and Belfast. These two unions numbered around 30,000 members each. Establishing a united organisation in all ports proved difficult, however, given that the nature of trade and labour organisation varied considerably from one location to another. Indeed, a separate South Side Labour Protection League was formed by dockers in London, representing the men employed in and around the Surrey Docks on the south bank of the Thames. The Tyneside and National Labour Union arose as a force in the north-east. And, of course, the gas workers and the railway workers continued to develop distinct organisations.

At the time there were those who regarded this as a major weakness. Will Thorne, for example, was disappointed that the docks strike did not advance the long-held vision of one big union for all general workers. Tillett and Mann preferred to focus on organising dockers alone at that stage, although they eventually agreed a scheme of mutual recognition of membership cards with the Gas Workers Union. Thorne's ambition of one general union remains unrealised 120 years later, alas.

As well as new organisations, there also developed a new spirit, represented in an advance of the perspective of socialism within the TUC, and a corresponding diminution of the previous commitment to Liberalism. This was reflected in a major victory for the 'new unionism' at the 1890 TUC, where the demand for legislation for an eight-hour working day was carried over the opposition of the movement's 'old guard', following a campaign which included a vast turnout at London's first May Day demonstration.

According to the Webbs:

> the victory of the London dockers and the impetus it gave to trade unionism throughout the country at last opened the eyes of the Trade Union world to the significance of the new movement. It was no longer possible for the Parliamentary Committee to denounce the Socialists as a set of outside intriguers.[9]

This victory meant that basic working-class demands for higher pay and shorter hours were placed at the heart of the agenda of the labour movement – and no longer for a craft elite, but for all working people. And while it would be wrong to exaggerate the move towards a more militant political perspective – gradualism was still more-or-less universally accepted among union leaders, and socialism remained a minority belief – there is no question but that broader perspectives on the place of labour in society were opening up. As Williams comments, the socialists and the new unionists were fighting for something much more important than the right to match their power against that of their employers: 'They were seeking to destroy a competitive system altogether divorced ... from social responsibilities and governed only by its own inner compulsions.'[10]

Engels surely had the perspective right when he argued that the revival of the East End of London was more important than 'this momentary fashion among bourgeois circles of affecting a mild dilution of Socialism' – and was more important even than the progress Socialism had made in England generally.[11]

Nor were gender relationships overlooked – appropriately, since it had been the women employed by Bryant and May who had led the movement towards new unionism. Ben Tillett himself expressed advanced views in a pamphlet on socialism:

> I see the time when men and women shall be equal. I see the time when the economic position of the woman shall be assured, when she shall be the possessor of her own body; of her own soul, when she shall be the mother of a great nation. I see when men shall respect womanhood.[12]

Formation of the Labour Party

Naturally, neither employers nor government took these developments lightly, presenting as they did a challenge to the capitalists' assumed divine right to rule in the factory and the country alike. A sustained offensive by the port employers, for example, had reduced the new unions to a shadow of their former selves by the mid-1890s. However, areas of strong organisation remained among both the dockers and the gas workers.

The full weight of the law was generally deployed against trade unionists, at least when they resorted to industrial action. This, combined with the gradual spread of socialist ideas within the working class, increasingly impelled trade unions towards a more active consideration of questions of political action, with some of the general unions to the fore. As Ken Coates explains, the political struggle was absolutely essential for the poorest people because they lacked the monopoly position of skilled workers. 'They could not trade on their scarcity. Instead they had to secure some political intervention to make space for recognition.'[13]

The earliest enduring stage in this growth of socialist ideas in the labour movement was the formation of the Independent Labour Party in 1893; however, most trade unions remained outside this initiative, and most trade unionists continued to support Liberal candidates in elections. The first steps taken towards a more comprehensive approach came with the formation of the Labour Representation Committee in 1900 on the initiative of the TUC. The LRC became the Labour Party in 1906. The Dockers' Union took part in this initiative, which brought together trade unions and socialist organisations to present common election candidates, though initially this was only in a minority of parliamentary constituencies. While most socialist groups affiliated to the new Labour Party, the party was not itself a socialist body. Its priority was the more limited objective of labour representation. Another trend that resonates through the T&G's subsequent history was established from the outset: though the unions dominated the new party organisationally and financially, they were by and large content to leave the political leadership to the parliamentarians.

The most notorious of the judicial attacks on trade unionism was the Taff Vale judgment of 1901, which came about as a result of a dispute on the railways in South Wales. The effect of this judgement was to remove the immunity of trade unions from being sued by employers for damages arising from industrial action by their members (whether authorised by the union or not). Since the damages sought were frequently punitively high, the effect of this judgment was to render effective trade unionism impossible. Repealing this law therefore became a central priority for the trade union movement, but the Liberal Party, tied as it was to the employing interests, proved highly dilatory in addressing the issue.

A further legal blow, aimed directly at the emerging political work of the unions, was the Osborne judgment. Once again, the Law Lords defied legal expectations by handing down a ruling which made all political activity by trade unions illegal, and limited unions to operating within the most restrictive possible interpretations of existing legislation. As with the Taff Vale judgment, the Liberal government was in no haste to right the wrong, which therefore remained on the statute book until 1913.

These political challenges to trade unionism unfolded in an

atmosphere of sharply heightened struggle in the years before the First World War. This touched dockers and other transport workers, of course. By 1911 the working and living conditions of dockers were once more sinking towards pre-1889 levels.

The principal unions organising in different forms of transport (all three dozen of them) united in 1910 into the National Transport Workers Federation on the initiative of the Dockers' Union. The next year there were big strikes in almost every port. In Liverpool the dockers were joined by the railway workers in stopping work, bringing that great city to a halt for a month, during which it was placed under military occupation.

The government tried to break the disputes through state repression and violence, but it was forced to back down by the solidarity of the working class. Indeed, for the first time since the heyday of the Chartist movement in the 1840s, the idea of a general strike was widely canvassed. In 1912 more than forty million working days were lost to strikes, up from less than three million just three years earlier. Not only dockers and railway workers, but also building workers and engineers were involved in this wave of action, which gives the lie to any rosy view of the Edwardian era as one of balmy increasing prosperity.

The outbreak of war in 1914 brought an end to this movement. The appeal of jingoism led many to abandon their allegiance to the internationalism of socialism and this led to a stalling of the forward advance of organised labour, politically and industrially.

Most British socialists and almost all trade union leaders hurried to support the government's war effort, mainly by promoting a regime of industrial peace. Ben Tillett, alas, was among those who lent assistance to military recruitment campaigns, after initially holding out against the chauvinistic war mood. Such an outlook by union leaders not only assisted in sending thousands of young men to be slaughtered, but also gave a powerful boost to employers' profits for the duration.

In Ireland, however, there was there was little of this patriotic class collaboration. Militant trade unionism was starting to fuse, under the leadership of Jim Larkin and James Connolly, with a national struggle which saw a majority of the Irish people demand their independence from Britain. The Irish Transport and General Workers Union founded by these two great leaders had already survived the Dublin Lock-Out of 1913, which saw 80,000 workers defy employers and state terror (with the help of solidarity from British trade unionists) in a struggle for the most basic rights. Though the strikers had been starved and beaten back to work, the lock-out had laid the foundations of general trade unionism in what is now the Irish Republic.

The war years saw a considerable abatement in the level of industrial action. And when a revival began, it was not concentrated in the transport industries for the most part, but among skilled engineering workers and coal miners. Coates and Topham present a balanced picture of the transport unions' work during the 1914-18 conflict. They acknowledge that the unions participated in the industrial truce, and 'failed to defend wage rates against rising inflation', but note that they also maintained a defence of labour's civil liberties, a critical attitude to employer profiteering and a cautious approach to the militarisation of industry. Certainly, transport union leaders such as Ernie Bevin and Robert Williams made use of the opportunity of war to extend trade union authority over labour supply (although they opposed Labour's participation in Lloyd George's war cabinet from 1916 on). And as the slaughter in the trenches dragged on without end in sight, domestic dissent on the war multiplied.[14]

Ernest Bevin

Here we should turn to a consideration of the role of Bevin, the first of the legendary trade union leaders associated with the T&G. Of course, many others played their part in bringing the plan for one union covering transport and general industries to fruition. But Bevin's role was decisive in the amalgamation process, as we shall see.

Ernest Bevin was born in Somerset in 1881 into a labouring family. His own early working life was spent as a carter in Bristol (Ben Tillett's home town), and it was there that he first developed an interest in trade unionism and socialism. Tillett's Dockers' Union was a considerable force in trade unionism in the south-west and South Wales, and its reach stretched far beyond the docks themselves into other industries. It was natural enough, therefore, that when Bevin started to organise the carters in Bristol it was within the Dockers' Union. In 1911 he started his career as a trade union official when he joined the staff of its Bristol office. It was from this base that he eventually became the most influential British trade unionist of the first half of the last century, utilising his growing influence in both the Dockers' Union and the Transport Workers Federation to promote the amalgamation that became the T&G.

Concerning Bevin's character and outlook, at least as it was when he emerged into a leading role in the labour movement at the close of the First World War, his biographer Alan Bullock offers this sketch:

> He had been set to learn in a rough school and the experience toughened his character. It had also deepened his hostility to the economic and social system under which he lived: he hated its exploitation, its injustice and its inequality. But the cast of his mind was practical rather than revolutionary and utopian. Instinctively he turned to organisation rather than agitation …
>
> He had no illusions about the employers: they would only listen to working-class demands when they were backed by organised power. But he had no illusions about his own side either: he had seen how easily ignorance, envy and suspicion could obscure common interests, how much energy the trade unions spent in

fighting each other. The working-class movement, for all its militant talk, would only become powerful when it had overcome the conflicts of interest within its own ranks.[15]

During the war Bevin rose within the ranks of his union, and also played a growing part in the Transport Workers Federation. After taking the opportunity to travel to the United States as part of a delegation, he returned impressed by the development of union organisation there. He increasingly began to operate on the national rather than local stage.

Labour after the war

Two factors in particular led to the reorganisation of trade unionism after the war – of which the formation of the T&G was a major part. The first was the rapid upturn in militancy, in an atmosphere of continent-wide social dislocation and revolutionary upheaval. Capitalism was being challenged as never before, and the position of ruling classes had never appeared weaker (although in Britain it retained greater resources than elsewhere in Europe). Secondly, and flowing from this circumstance, there was a growing understanding that the existing working-class organisations were not entirely fit for the new era.

That era was marked by an immense upsurge in strikes. In 1919, the year in which socialist revolution seemed imminent in Germany, Hungary and elsewhere in Europe, Britain 'lost' nearly 35 million days to industrial action (as against under six million the previous year). By 1921 the figure had risen to over 85 million! The *New Statesman* reflected the changed mood:

The greatest barrier to labour unrest before the war was the widespread conviction that capitalism was inevitable – that it had been in possession ever since the workers could remember, and that there were no signs that it was likely to come to an end. Today, the world, and the workers perhaps most of all, have lost the feeling of certainty about anything.[16]

This was above all the consequence of the successful Russian revolution, which for the first time brought an avowedly socialist government to power. The British government was, in Churchill's words, determined to do what it could to 'strangle Bolshevism at birth'.

The working-class movement, by contrast, was broadly sympathetic to the Russian revolution, and when Lloyd George's government sought to arm Polish armies invading Russia, Bevin was to the fore in mobilising labour opinion to act in opposition to any such support: 'We are ready and determined to resist the triumph of reaction and war ... It is not merely a political action, but an action representing the full force of Labour and we believe it represents the desire of the great majority of the British people'. This culminated in London dockers refusing to handle the *Jolly George*, a ship with munitions bound for Poland. Bevin's justification for this action speaks eloquently of his political view of trade unionism at the time and, like much else he said and did, has contemporary relevance:

> I was glad that when the London dockers realized that the *Jolly George* was to go to Poland with munitions, they absolutely refused to load her ... I was not going to ask the dockers to put a gun in a ship or to carry on these further wicked ventures and wars among people in the East ... I think the working people ... have a right to say where their labour and how their labour shall be used, and if we are being called upon either to make munitions or transport munitions for purposes which outrage our sense of justice, then I think we have a right to refuse to have our labour prostituted to carry on wars of this character.[17]

Labour had struggles enough at home, of course. The new mood also affected the Labour Party: it embraced socialism – at least in formal terms – with the adoption of Clause Four of the party's constitution (drafted by eminent Fabians Sidney and Beatrice Webb), committing itself to the public ownership of the means of production, distribution and exchange. And a 'Triple Alliance' was established of the miners, transport workers and railway workers to oppose employers' attempts to meet the post-war economic difficulties by attacks on workers' wages and conditions, an attack that was particularly fierce in the mining industry.

Indeed, revolution was in the air. Prime Minister Lloyd George recognised as much when he told a delegation from the triple alliance, then on the point of united strike action:

> We are at your mercy ... If you carry out your threat and strike, then you will defeat us. But if you do so ... have you weighed the consequences ... For, if a force arises in the state which is stronger than the state itself, then it must be ready to take on the functions of the state, or it must withdraw and accept the authority of the state. Gentlemen, are you ready?

It was as succinct a presentation of the revolutionary question as has ever been given. The leaders of the Triple Alliance were, of course, not ready at all, having no perspective for assuming state power. The strike failed to materialise after the government conceded on most of the alliance's demands (an end to conscription and military intervention in Soviet Russia; and no military interference in industrial disputes), but the state lived to fight another day – and before long at that.

The fledgling MI5 was sending alarming reports to the Cabinet about the mood of the working class. Factors stimulating revolutionary feeling were many: profiteering and high prices; poor housing; 'the foolish and dangerous ostentation of the rich'; unemployment; and also education by Labour Colleges, the circulation of the Labour press and Marxist literature and 'the influence of extremist trade union leaders'. Countervailing factors were limited to two – the popularity of the Royal Family and of sport.[18]

The state security service was not being unduly alarmist – just two years later Ernest Bevin concluded his first report to the T&G executive with the ringing declaration that 'great unions like our own can make a great contribution to ... development, both industrially and politically – we urge great comradeship, a supreme effort to secure the passing of real power from the master class to the working class.' Even trade union leaders now remembered as 'moderate' were in the early 1920s militant well beyond the standards of contemporary left-wingers!

Shaw Inquiry

It was conditions in the docks, however, that were to provide fresh impetus towards the development of what became the T&G, and for the first time to bring Bevin to national prominence.

The position of the dockers had not improved to any great extent since 1889. Poverty wages and casual work remained their lot in most ports, where they were at the mercy of the ebb and flow of trade and rapacious employers alike. Jack Banfield, a turn-of-the-century London docker, describes the consequences of the prevailing casualisation:

> Now you never knew whether it was going to be half a day, one day, or a week's work. Medland Wharf used to have a system where they had some little brass tallies, and if they gave you a brass tally you were employed. The thing was, when you got that brass tally in your hand, you had to grab it quick, because if you didn't what used to happen was that someone would knock it out, away would go your brass tally, and whoever picked that brass tally up got the day's work.[19]

Endeavouring to stabilise the post-war social turmoil, Lloyd George's government established an enquiry headed by Lord Shaw to look into conditions in the docks in 1920. This was at a moment when the unions were relatively strong, with ninety per cent organisation in the ports – before the slump in world trade that weakened them once more. It was at this enquiry that Bevin, who had been chosen by the NTWF to put the workers' case, earned his reputation as the Dockers' QC.

His opening presentation highlighting the dockers' demand for a living wage took more than two days, drawing on the most painstaking research into actual conditions in ports all over the country. It was a presentation with a clear class edge, highlighting as it did (in spite of resistance from Lord Shaw) the huge profits employers were making, and one with a considerable element of PR flair.

When a Cambridge academic named Bowley, giving evidence for the employers, asserted that a dockers' family of five could live on £3.63 per week – the unions were claiming £6 for such a family – Bevin (or, according to other accounts, his secretary) went shopping in an East London market on Bowley's budget. He then theatrically displayed the meagre results, pressing the witness as to whether he – never mind a worker engaged in hard manual toil – could manage to survive on such fare.

Could you live on this? Bevin cooks on a dockers' wage

But Bevin's docker was not expected to live on food alone, however much of it might be supplied. Bevin's opening address is also celebrated for its location of the dockers' economic case in a far broader setting:

> If your Court refuse our claim I suggest that you must adopt an alternative. You must go to the Prime Minister ... and tell him to close our schools, tell him that industry can only be run by artisan labour on the pure fodder or animal basis, teach us nothing, let us learn nothing, because to create aspirations in our minds, to create the love of the beautiful and then at the same time to deny us the wherewithal to obtain it is a false policy ... Better keep us in dark ignorance, never to know anything, if you are going to refuse us the wherewithal to give expression to those aspirations which have thus been created.[20]

Shaw came out against casual labour in the docks – the next step in a journey towards full decasualisation which was not, however, to be

Ernie Bevin and Ben Tillet at the Shaw Enquiry

completed for another generation – and a wage rate of sixteen shillings (80p) per day. Bevin was feted at a celebratory rally at the Albert Hall for his efforts. And it was clear that the main thrust of his arguments – which combined moral force with detailed research and presentation – were not solely applicable to dockers. They were a charter for general unionism's principles.

Amalgamation

The post-war circumstances had highlighted the weaknesses of existing trade union organisation, including that of the National Transport Workers Federation, which, as is often the case with federations reserving considerable authority to their component parts, found it hard to act in the swift and determined way that events sometimes required. This increasingly compelled the more far-sighted trade unionists to seek another way forward – amalgamation.

The original hope was to bring all transport unions – docks, road (passenger and commercial), maritime and rail – into one single union. That proved over-ambitious, however, and in the end negotiations centred around nineteen different unions, based in docks and in road transport. An amalgamation committee was formed and, amid the industrial turmoil of 1921, a proposal was put forward for a new union, to be placed before the members of the individual unions.

Bevin and Harry Gosling were respectively chairman and secretary of the Amalgamation Committee – and the driving forces in the whole process. The text of the message from these two that accompanied the papers for the ballot has become one of the more celebrated documents in British trade union history, doubtless because of the enduring relevance of its central message. It is therefore worth citing in full:

Fellow Workers:-

The great scheme of amalgamation will be submitted to you for ballot forthwith.

The scheme has received considered judgment of the Executives of each union that are parties to it, and at a great delegate conference in London it was endorsed unanimously.

We are convinced that this is the right step to take to secure the necessary power and efficiency to deal with the problems that must be solved by the Movement.

Our unions have, in their respective sections, played a wonderful part in the past, but PROGRESS DEMANDS that existing methods shall give way to new.

CAPITAL IS WELL ORGANISED – EVERY TRADE IS INTERWOVEN AND INTERLINKED.

The great industries on the employers' side stand together!! Labour must do likewise. Whoever stands in the Way of this great change in methods of organisation is doing a grave injustice not only to the present generation, but to the children yet unborn! The scheme allows for the creation of a GREAT and POWERFUL UNION.

It pools its financial resources.

It gives opportunity to create efficient methods of negotiation and handling disputes.

It gets rid of jealousy between Unions.

It allows the rank and file to co-operate in port, waterway, road transport and factory.

It gives the officials greater scope; a greater opportunity of acquiring knowledge – placing them on an equal footing with employers in dealing with your problems.

It provides for each section to have its own National Committee.

It allows opportunity to shape its own programme and policy, at the same time bringing to the assistance of any one section both the moral and financial strength of the remainder.

It proposes to organise the whole of the workers engaged in the respective industries covered by the new Union – administrative, clerical and manual.

It is the creation of a NEW MACHINE.

It will ultimately not only talk of wages, but exercise greater
power and control.

WE MOST EARNESTLY APPEAL TO EVERY MEMBER OF
THE AMALGAMATING UNIONS TO SECURE THEIR
BALLOT PAPER AND UTILISE THEIR VOTE IN ITS FAVOUR.

NOTHING CAN PREVENT IT – only two things can hinder it –
namely – VESTED INTEREST and APATHY.

If vested interest stands in its way, then vested interest will be
swept aside by force of events.

If, owing to apathy of the rank and file, the necessary power is not
given to the Committee to go on immediately, then the RANK
AND FILE WILL BE GUILTY of a crime against themselves, their
wives and their children.

It is said it's the duty *of Leaders to lead – We now give you the lead
– Don't fail to respond!!*

This resonant appeal secured the desired result in fourteen of
the unions that were ultimately balloted. The stevedores' and the
Scottish dockers' unions were among those which either voted
against the proposal or failed to secure the minimum 50 per cent
turnout required by law, although the latter was brought within the
T&G (temporarily) before long. The slogan of 'One Big Union'
under which amalgamation rallies were held across the country
clearly struck a chord with workers who were fed up with the
limitations of many little unions.

Following a rules conference in Leamington and the election of
Gosling, Bevin and Stanley Hirst to their posts as President,
General Secretary and Financial Secretary respectively, the way was
now clear for the Transport and General Workers Union to come
into the world, from January 1 1922.[21]

Bevin's election was a foregone conclusion, given the central part
he had played in the amalgamation. Nevertheless, his election
address was terse to the point of rudeness. It consisted of this alone:
'Just as I have given of my best in the past in all offices I have held in

The graphic case for trade union unity

the movement, so shall I continue if the membership repose renewed confidence in me in a new post.' Challenged by two other candidates, Bevin won 96,842 votes, while his rivals received just over 10,000 votes between them – certainly the highest ratio of votes to manifesto words in T&G election history. In his election appeal one of his opponents, London docks official Fred Thompson, did, however, anticipate later criticisms of Bevin. He said that his own candidacy was 'a challenge to autocracy and a protest against the building up of a new Union round individuals instead of policy'.[22]

The T&G in 1922

Right from the beginning the T&GWU was, of course, more than just a dockers' union. In the years before 1922 road transport workers had been going through their own often-painful process of organisation, alliance and merger. The London busworkers, for example, had found themselves as a left-wing minority in the United Vehicle Workers Union as a result of a merger in 1920. One of their leaders, George Sanders, actually expressed doubts about joining up with the T&G because, as he wrote in the *UVW Record*, 'the officials of some of the unions that we are asked to amalgamate with went over to the side of the capitalist class while the late war was in progress ... there is no guarantee that in the face of a crisis they would not do exactly the same again.'[23]

Nevertheless, the UVW did take part in the great amalgamation, as its main passenger transport element, and it provided the early T&G with two of its most important officials under Bevin – Stanley Hirst and John Cliff. These unions of course had their own record of struggle. To take but one example, the whole issue of equal pay for women workers, a thread which runs throughout the union's history, first came to the fore in the 1918 London bus strike. However, the question was not adequately pursued by the NTWF at the time.

The National Union of Vehicle Workers represented road haulage workers in the amalgamation, although the United Road Transport

Union stayed outside the T&G, and remains in existence as a separate union to this day.

Bevin's Dockers' Union had itself extended its sphere of organisation beyond the docks. It had a considerable number of branches in the milling industry, as well as including clerical workers and those in an eclectic variety of other trades. Much of the membership in South Wales, for example, was in the tinplate industry. And Bevin himself, as we have seen, had been a carter rather than a docker. Even before the formation of the T&G, the concept of 'general unionism' was sinking deep roots. Tony Topham explained why docks unions were naturally drawn towards expansion into other industries:

> First, there was the need to exclude all potential blacklegs from strike-breaking in the casual labour industries such as transport ... because all non-unionists were potential blacklegs who would break their strikes. So immediately they went out to recruit agricultural labourers, carters, in South Wales the tinplate men, factory and mill labourers everywhere ... The second purpose was to overcome sectionalism.[24]

However, if the T&G as created was more than a dockers' union, it was also less than the comprehensive all-transport union which Bevin and his colleagues had hoped for. The seafarers' union declined to join and, despite high hopes at the T&G's founding conference, so also did the railway unions, of which the NUR was the most important. This proved to be a considerable industrial handicap through the succeeding years. Now known as the RMT, the railway workers' union again remains a separate organisation down to the present. Indeed, despite the enormous decline in employment in that industry, the three railway trade unions have yet to merge with each other, never mind with any larger union.

Nor, indeed, were all dockers to join the T&G in 1922, or for some time afterwards. The London stevedores and lightermen were to maintain separate unions for many years to come, a fact which was often a source of friction. Glasgow dockers were out of the amalgamation, then in and then out again, while many dockers in the north-east ports were in the General & Municipal Workers Union. However, it is fair to say that, with only local exceptions, the T&G dominated dockside trade unionism from its inception.

Bringing fourteen unions with around 350,000 members together was, of course, task enough, and most of those who have studied the matter concur that it could not have been achieved without Bevin's combination of vision, firmness and tact. This latter quality was particularly needed when dealing with the difficulties of conciliating the ambitions and interests of fourteen different union general secretaries, each accustomed to running their own show and now required to sink their ambitions into the larger enterprise. Finding a position for the legendary Ben Tillett, still leader of the Dockers' Union and seething at being superseded by his talented protégé, was particularly difficult. In the end, he was named the union's international and political secretary and found a seat as a Labour MP, although this was not enough to prevent further upset some years later when he was finally forced to retire at the age of 71.

Bevin's touch in handling people seldom failed him at this stage, his attempt in 1924 to remove Harry Gosling from the union's presidency being an exception. After this move failed, Gosling remained the union's first and only full-time President until retirement in 1930.[25]

It was Bevin who designed the structure of the T&G, combining national trade groups for each industry in which the new union organised with a large measure of regional decentralisation. There were initially six national trade groups, each headed by a committee of lay members and serviced by a full-time national secretary. Bevin himself combined the role of national secretary for the docks with his job as T&G general secretary, reflecting the importance of dockers to the new union and the pressing industrial problems in the ports. The other trade groups were waterways, passenger transport, commercial road transport, clerical, and general, the last-named uniting those sections of the membership deemed not to require a trade group of their own. Of these six groups five were still extant in 2008, waterways being the exception – it had long-since merged with the docks group.

There were from the outset industrial sections of the membership not given national trade groups of their own. Right from the start the T&G had footholds in the developing chemical industry and, as noted, in metals. Here were the seeds of future trade groups. These non-transport workers were somewhat aggrieved at being grouped together as 'general' in 1922. Sub-sections within the General Workers Trade groups were created to allow a measure of industrial expression to these diverse groups, without allowing space for this to develop into a broader sectionalism. The 'general' trade group spun off many further trade groups down the years, but was still there at the merger with Amicus, organising workers in cleaning, paper production, construction materials and other sectors. The white-collar group (ACTSS) was initially mainly for clerks in the port industry, but local government workers were also organised in Bristol, giving the T&G a public service element from the beginning.

The union also established eleven regions (called areas until after World War Two, but for clarity referred to by their present name throughout this work), a total which later rose to thirteen, before reducing back to the original eleven and finally to eight. Again these were led by lay committees and supported by a regional secretary, a post which provided a berth for many of the displaced general secretaries of the merging unions. The regional boundaries did not in all cases correspond to the conventional regions into which England is divided (Scotland, Ireland and Wales constituted a separate region at this stage) but rather followed industrial requirements and membership patterns. Thus the midlands, east and west, constituted a single region. Region number one, the T&G's largest throughout its history, covered not just London and the Home Counties but much of East Anglia and the south-east. On the other hand, region number ten consisted of just Hull and a few smaller east coast ports; while region two comprised Southampton, Portsmouth and their hinterland, plus the Channel Islands. Each region had its own regional trade group committees corresponding to the national committees. These regional trade group committees elected representatives both to their local regional committee and to the national committee of their group. From the outset the T&G had a national officer responsible for women workers, but several generations were to elapse before a national women's committee was established.

There was flexibility in this structure from the beginning – in Wales, there were no regional trade groups but district committees instead, while in Ireland there were neither, with all work led by the regional committee. At Central Office in London there was a general organising department (as well as legal, international/political and financial departments).

Atop this structure was the General Executive Council (GEC), consisting entirely of lay members, with no full-time official allowed to serve, a marked difference from the situation in many other unions at the time. The GEC included both regional representatives elected by ballot and trade group representatives, one being elected by each national committee. While the union's biennial conference was the ultimate authority on policy, it was the GEC that had charge of the running of the union and the supervision of its industrial business. And the GEC itself was led by its general secretary – without a vote but able to exercise an enormous and usually decisive influence, never more so than when drafting the union's rules. Here Bevin held sway, always standing 'for the whole, and the centre, against the part and the parish'. He insisted on the Executive having the finally say in authorising strike action, and on Executive appointment of and control over all officials, rather than election, the latter procedure having proved open to abuse.[26]

As labour historian Allen Hutt put it, this was 'an ingenious structure – combining a high degree of centralisation with a double division of its members, vertically by industrial groups and horizontally by areas – [which] enabled this powerful body to be substantially dominated by its forceful general secretary, Mr Ernest Bevin'.[27]

Doubtless that formed part of Bevin's intentions. He was already developing the leadership style, sometimes known as 'popular bossdom', which was to become one of his hallmarks. Bevin saw a strong office of general secretary as the essential – indeed perhaps the only – guarantee of the union's global integrity, and of its ability to overcome the initially powerful pull of sectional interest. His structure permitted substantial regional and sectional scope as a way of overcoming regionalism and sectionalism, which without such flexibility could find expression

'We seek knowledge that we may wield power'

in industrial or local breakaways, or those which were a combination of both.

Whatever the mix of motives, the structure he designed has stood the test of time remarkably well. Right down to 2007, active T&G members remained for the most part attached to both their trade group and their region, and this fortified rather than undermined their solidarity with the union as a whole.

The eminence of trade groups is perhaps easier to understand – in a general union covering workers in a multiplicity of industries, a substantial degree of industrial autonomy is an unavoidable requirement, lest trade unionists in one smaller section feel that their own industrial business is being decided by others not directly affected. The regional structure reflected the diversity of conditions prevailing in the docks at the time, as well as the need to have powerful officials 'on the spot', able to resolve issues at a time when communications were relatively slow, at least by twenty-first century standards. The regions were responsible for work that could not easily be managed from the T&G's new headquarters in Westminster – organisation, recruitment and financial administration (at a time when cash was still very much king and membership records involved keeping track of large numbers of very small transactions). However, the survival of strong regional organisation also reflects the sense that democracy in a very big working-class organisation must involve a fair measure of decentralisation. The alternative is to have all decisions taken at a remote head office, beyond the effective control of the membership. Bevin created a structure which allowed the T&G to act locally while thinking nationally or even globally.

It was not a foregone conclusion that the T&G would survive. In the early years Bevin was continually exercised by the danger of breakaways from the union – fears that were not always without foundation. Membership also had a considerable tendency to fluctuation (employment in the docks being particularly sensitive to changes in the world trade position), and the union's finances

The new General Secretary rallies his members

were often under strain, not least because of the need to maintain on the payroll the large number of officials inherited from the amalgamating unions.

Yet survive it did. As Bevin told the T&G's first biennial delegate conference in 1923:

We live not for today, but for the future. Gosling, Tillett, Sexton and the others laid the foundations of this movement under difficult circumstances. The circumstances are different now. We have got to carry on – you and I – to another stage in upward development. That is our task in our day and generation and I beg of you, do not shirk it.[28]

Notes

1. Morton/Tate, p184.
2. McCarthy, p21.
3. Williams, p176.
4. Webbs, p390.
5. Williams, pp176-77.
6. McCarthy, p241.
7. Marx & Engels, p399.
8. Williams, p179.
9. Webbs, p393. 'Parliamentary Committee' was the contemporary term for what would become the TUC General Council.
10. Williams, p193-94.
11. Fox, p62.
12. T&G, p11.
13. Coates/Topham 2, p30.
14. Coates/Topham, pp570ff.
15. Bullock, p37.
16. Coates/Topham, p693.
17. Coates/Topham, pp746-7, 750.
18. Coates/Topham, pp716-20.
19. Weightman/Humphries, pp48-49.
20. Coates/Topham, p737.
21. Coates/Topham, pp809-11.
22. Coates/Topham, p843; Bullock, p198.
23. Fuller, p65.
24. Coates/Topham 2, p14.
25. Allen, p79.
26. Coates/Topham, p829.
27. Hutt, p91.
28. T&GWU report on First Biennial Delegate Conference.

2. General strike and depression 1923–1939

W hile it was still in its infancy Bevin's creation was tested severely. The T&G drew its first industrial breath during an economic slump, and at a time when unemployment was high. The new union was losing members even while the balloting on amalgamation was proceeding. Early results – in terms of improvements for the membership – were therefore hard to come by. The union had barely been established before Bevin was acquiescing in a wage reduction in the docks. This decision prompted a prolonged unofficial strike in London and Hull, which caused divisions that were to overshadow the T&G's first delegate conference, threatening to split the union at birth. Many dockers took the view that 'Bevin had no guts for a fight … he had sold out to the bosses.'[1]

Bevin's defence was that if trade unionism was to have a future in industrial relations, the union had to reach the best deal it could in the circumstances and then abide by the agreement. These were themes that were to guide his activity as a union leader over the next twenty years. Bevin also retrieved his position on this occasion by leading a successful docks strike in 1924, which forced the employers to concede a two shillings a day pay increase, and a further enquiry into decasualisation. And the T&G greeted the arrival of Ramsay MacDonald's first minority Labour government with a strike on London Tramways, which ended with a six shillings a week pay increase. So Bevin's actions may have roused the suspicion of some of the union's more militant members, but the press was starting to turn the T&G leader into 'the most hated and most abused man in the country' – a title borne with honour by many trade unionists since.[2]

These early battles were only symptoms of a broader condition – the class struggle was acute in the early 1920s, in Britain as in the rest of Europe. Working people were unwilling to accept a return to pre-war conditions, and felt betrayed by the failure of government to deliver on war-time promises of a 'land fit for heroes'. The establishment, for its part, was determined to restore and defend its social privileges, in an atmosphere coloured by the fear of Bolshevism and the successful revolution in Russia. This dramatic period in British social history culminated in the General Strike of 1926, a central event in the development of the trade union movement.

The broad story of the strike is well known. The dispute had its origin in the coal owners' desire to cut the already low wages paid to their miners, and/or to lengthen their working day. In this they were supported by the Conservative government of the time, headed by Stanley Baldwin (with Winston Churchill as a particularly aggressive anti-union Chancellor). In 1925, political pressure forced the owners to back down from their demands, but the breathing space thus secured was used by employers and the state to make the most careful preparations to win the coming confrontation. These included jailing the leadership of the Communist Party – the most militant section of the movement – so that they could play no direct part in influencing events. Some may see this as a sign of British moderation – in 1919 the German establishment had simply murdered Communist leaders Karl Liebknecht and Rosa Luxemburg.

The TUC, alas, took no corresponding initiatives in readiness for the inevitable resumption of hostilities. When the government subsidy which had secured temporary peace ran out in May 1926, the rapacious coal-owners returned to the offensive and locked the miners out for their refusal to accept an extra hour on the working day as well as pay cuts. The TUC General Council called a general strike in support of the miners, and millions of workers struck solidly for nine days in the face of increasing state violence. But the General Council then called off the strike with absolutely nothing gained; the TUC was unwilling to confront the fundamental issues of power in society that the strike raised. The majority of the union leadership was, ultimately, more afraid of the consequences of defeating the government than of losing the strike. The miners were left to fight on alone, to be starved back to work in one area after another in the ensuing months. It was not until the Second World War that trade unionism could be said to have recovered from this dispute, and to a certain extent the negative legacy of the General Strike was not fully laid to rest until the big struggles of the early 1970s.

The 353,000 members of the T&G were among those supporting the miners, bringing docks and transport to a halt (notwithstanding the very token efforts of middle-class scabs to run trams and buses in some places). The union paid out nearly £300,000 in dispute benefit, an immense sum for the time – something which bore heavily in Bevin's calculations.

The *British Worker*, the newspaper published by the TUC while Fleet Street was shut down by the strike, carried the T&G's bulletins on the response of its membership, giving a flavour of the struggle:

> London and Home Counties Area: At their own request, cab drivers are ceasing work. The position with regard to all sections in the area is well maintained. Waterways are exceptionally solid, and the Woolwich Free Ferry has been stopped for the first time in history. Effective steps are being taken to counter the attempts of the London County Council to institute a passenger service with the aid of volunteers.
>
> Midlands Area: reports from all districts most satisfactory. Attempts to run bus service failed.
>
> North-West Coast Area: Attempts to run a Manchester tramway service abandoned …

Scottish Area ... absolutely solid. The members of the street passenger service have stood as one man.

North of England Area ... Attempts to run passenger services have been frustrated.

North Midlands and Yorkshire Area ... Tramways at a standstill. Steps are being taken to deal with 'unrecognised' bus services.

South of England Area: With the exception of tramwaymen in Southampton (20 per cent working) and Portsmouth (125 men working), all sections remain solid.

West of England Area ... The spirit at present displayed is beyond anything witnessed in past years.

South Wales Area ... Attempts to circulate false rumours amongst men in outlying districts have been successfully scotched. The statements broadcast yesterday to the effect that Cardiff Docks are working were found to be absolutely untrue.

East Coast Area ... No cargo is being handled in the docks throughout the area. The number of strikers considerably increased yesterday, due to many employers endeavouring to introduce blackleg labour.[3]

After the dispute the union's journal, the *Record*, editorialised as follows:

On the first day of the strike practically the whole of our members were involved. The loyalty and enthusiasm with which they answered the call have earned for them a golden page in the history of our union. The lesson labour has learned is that the solidarity of the working class must be demonstrated in another field of activity. On the industrial field labour staggered its masters. When it gets a chance on the political field it will deliver the knock-out blow.

*On the march during
the General Strike*

Bevin's role in the strike was important. He played a leading part in all the deliberations of the General Council, to which he had only recently been elected. He was dismayed at the unions' lack of preparations for the confrontation, and he soon came to a pragmatic view that the strike was not going to be won. While not aligned with the complete capitulators on the General Council's right-wing, he was not prepared to lead a militant fight for victory, involving calling out further groups of workers. In the words of a left-wing historian, he 'feared even more that the strikers, the working class, might win in a revolutionary fashion'. However, of the TUC delegation that met Prime Minister Baldwin to throw in the towel, he was the only one to at least attempt to seek guarantees (which were not given) on addressing the problem of the miners and resisting the victimisation of strikers.[4]

Bevin's own view of the outcome was bleak. On the day of the surrender he said: '... the best way to describe today ... is that we have committed suicide. Thousands of members will be victimised as the result of this day's work.'[5]

Indeed they were. Fifteen hundred T&G members, mostly leading activists, were persecuted after the strike, unable to return to their jobs as the government and the employers seized on the TUC's feebleness to launch a full-scale assault on trade union organisation.

After the strike

Strikes diminished rapidly in number after 1926. Over the next seven years an average four million days a year were lost to industrial action, and in the seven years beyond that the average fell further to less than two million days per year. Trade unionism was clearly in a new environment: one that was shaped by a legal assault from the government, who were determined that there should be no repetition of the revolutionary scare of 1926; by the growth of mass unemployment, particularly from 1929 onwards; and by a turn away from radicalism on the part of almost all the major unions. Left-wing influence in the unions began to diminish.

The Baldwin government introduced new restrictions on union's political activity and on the right to strike, although it is sobering to note that even under the 1927 legislation it was still permissible to undertake sympathetic action within one's own industry, something that would be unlawful today, after more than ten years of 'new' Labour government!

Trade union membership overall dropped to under five million and continued falling until 1934. Funds fell likewise, by around one-third. The T&G's membership dropped, and it had to cope with the consequences of having spent a small fortune during the General Strike, on dispute benefit and other costs. This left the union in no position to financially support a major strike for some time to come. But the decline in morale was even greater. The working-class solidarity which the strike had shown was undermined by feelings of betrayal and victimisation. According to Bevin's biographer Alan Bullock, the militant spirit which had characterised the unions in the years before 1926 had burned out.[6]

It was in this context that what was to be the first of many attempts to institutionalise a form of 'social partnership' in industry was undertaken, on the initiative of Alfred Mond, then the boss of giant chemicals company ICI. He wrote to the TUC urging talks on a range of industrial problems, arguing: 'we believe that the common interests which bind us are more powerful than the apparently divergent interests which seem to separate us'. A joint committee of representatives of the TUC and the Federation of British Industries (forerunner of today's CBI) was formed, and Bevin was included among its members. Although the talks led to very little in terms of concrete change beyond raising the self-esteem of the union leaders involved – another constant of social partnership schemes – it did seem, as Francis Williams has commented, that trade unionism was moving into an era of constructive participation, and being given status in fields of industrial policy where it had previously been denied.[7]

Bevin was representative of this change. Indeed, given his post-general strike eminence in the movement, he became one of its foremost advocates. To quote Williams: 'If the strike leader had formerly been the most characteristic figure of much of trade-union history ... the characteristic figure of this new age of trade unionism was the negotiator, the imaginative yet practical statesman of industry, of whom Bevin stands out as the most formidable and successful prototype.'[8]

Bevin took steps to carry the T&G with him along this new course. The union's General Executive Council held a special conference in 1927, at a large house owned by the Co-op in Woolwich, to discuss plans for recovery. Bevin outlined a new pragmatism under which, 'we have to deal with our business on business lines and whilst working under a capitalist system we have to have regard to it accordingly' – while being in principle committed to another form of society.[9]

The Workers' Union

In spite of these difficulties, the T&G continued to add members in this period through merger. By the end of 1926, thirteen additional unions (on top of the original fourteen) had joined the amalgamation; these included dockers in Glasgow (who were not to stay long), a Rotherham-based union of enginemen and mechanics, which formed the basis for a new trade group for Power Workers, and the North Wales quarrymen, whose accession, since they had been brought in with a promise of very wide autonomy within the T&G, led to the creation of a new union region in their own area. An agreement to merge with the GMWU – the holy grail of trade union amalgamations – was signed but then allowed to lapse, the first of many such false starts in that respect.[10]

The most important merger the T&G undertook during the 1920s was with the Workers' Union. The Workers' Union was another of Tom Mann's creations. Founded in 1898, its name expressed its intent. In Mann's words:

> The name was important. The idea was to have a short name yet genuinely comprehensive. 'The Workers' Union' was decided upon and it proved to be exactly the right name. It barred none; it welcomed all. It was wide, yet definite…[11]

Workers' Union membership grew rapidly during the war in the munitions and engineering industry, including among women workers entering the factories for the first time. The union organised in engineering, brewing and food processing, metal, rubber, agriculture, construction, municipal and government employment and elsewhere. It reached out to women workers on a significant scale – for example young organisers such as Ruby Part in Somerset extended trade unionism to glove-workers in rural areas. Membership of the Workers' Union peaked at around half a million in 1920, but it proved very vulnerable to the effects of slump – it was scattered in relatively small packets over hundreds of trades and industries, held together not by traditional industrial ties but by a large and expensive force of full-time organisers. Down to 140,000 members by 1923, the union faced growing financial and organisational problems; it was trying to operate outside both the T&G and the GMWU, and was generally in the difficult position of being only the second union in nearly all the fields in which it organised.[12]

Continuing widespread unemployment, the cost of the General Strike and a series of financial misjudgements (including unaffordable benefits) placed further pressure on the union as an independent entity. Finally, in 1929, with its membership down to just 100,000, it was forced to consider merger with the T&G as the only way to secure its future. After talks with Bevin yielded an acceptable plan, the Workers' Union membership endorsed amalgamation in a ballot, by 59,801 to 9,632.[13]

This merger was significant for the T&G in several ways. Firstly, it gave the union a much-needed membership boost and helped to break the general spiral of decline which had set in since 1926. Still more consequentially, it established the T&G as a force in industrial sectors where it had hitherto been peripheral, from engineering to agriculture. At the end of a transitional period, in 1931, a large element of the Workers' Union membership transferred into the T&G's new Metal, Engineering and Chemical Trade Group, leaving the union well placed to grow in those modern industries when an economic upturn eventually arrived – industries that were less vulnerable than the docks to world trade fluctuations. The first national secretary of this new group, Andrew Dalgleish, and its first representative on the T&G executive, Fred Hobbs, both came from the Workers' Union. So too did three consecutive Women's Officers – Julia Varley, Florence Hancock and Ellen McCullough. The merger also doubled the size of the General Workers Trade Group. Nearly one hundred new full-time officers had to be absorbed by the T&G, but this was no more than a passing difficulty.[14]

Welcome to the Workers' Union

The Workers' Union merger was certainly one which played an immense part in shaping the subsequent development of the T&G – indeed, the latter may never have become Britain's largest trade union without the entrance to new areas of industry that it afforded. As Topham remarks, 'without the merger of the Workers' Union in 1929, the TGWU might well have had a narrower history, and have been unable to assert its senior and numerical dominance in the car industry, aircraft, chemicals and so on.' Certainly, it put the 'General' on an equal footing with the 'Transport' in the T&G.[15]

1929–31 Labour government

Labour returned to office in 1929. Ramsey MacDonald found himself heading a minority government once more, but this time with a much larger body of MPs than in 1924, and, on the surface at least, a more ambitious programme of social reform.

Little of this was to materialise, but one piece of legislation important to the T&G was passed – the Road Transport Act 1930, piloted by Herbert Morrison, which provided for the co-ordination of the licensing of passenger transport across the country. The union fell out with Morrison, however, over the latter's resistance to putting any union representatives on the London Passenger Transport Board (he preferred 'experts'); this row marked the beginning of the long-standing animosity between Bevin and Morrison, a feud which persisted throughout their later service in government together.

Whatever good intentions MacDonald may have had in 1929 – and he was already showing signs of preferring the company of duchesses to that of working people – the great capitalist crisis which broke that same year put paid to them. The worldwide slump which followed the Wall Street crash raised questions which could only have been answered by real socialist change, something well beyond the ken of the Prime Minister and his Chancellor Phillip Snowden. Snowden was wedded to a Treasury orthodoxy that prioritised balancing the national books, and maintaining the value of the pound and export earnings. This was a time when British social democracy had forgotten whatever Marx it knew, and had not yet encountered Keynes.

The crisis sent unemployment soaring, as factories, mills and mines closed down and large industrial areas of the country became all but derelict. The determination of MacDonald and Snowden to resolve the crisis by imposing further hardships on the working class (in particular through reducing the already meagre level of unemployment assistance), rather than by challenging City priorities, led to a split in the government. MacDonald, Snowden and a small handful of others (among them Jimmy Thomas, leader of the railway workers' union) abandoned Labour to form a 'national government', which was entirely dominated by the Tories from the outset.

Throughout this period the T&G stayed loyal to the Labour Party, thereby ensuring that this sensational betrayal did not lead to the party's destruction, although the subsequent parliamentary election, held in an atmosphere of crisis, reduced it to a parliamentary rump, with few seats remaining outside mining districts. Bevin played the leading part in rallying affiliated unions to the party and preventing them following MacDonald, who retained considerable personal influence as one of Labour's historic leaders. As a result of this, he gained a stature in the political wing of the movement similar to that he had achieved within the TUC following the General Strike. In 1926, 1931 and again in 1940, the T&G's leader proved himself particularly powerful in a crisis.

Crisis years

The 1930s are remembered as the hardest of times for working people in Britain and Ireland. Yet this picture, while broadly true of course, conceals a diversity of industrial circumstances that vary from one sector of the economy and region of the country to another. As the economy showed the first signs of recovering from the 1929-32 slump, new industries began to develop in the Midlands and the south, while older industrial areas, particularly those dependent on coal mining and shipbuilding, like the north-east and South Wales, remained mired in depression and dereliction. So opportunities for the T&G to organise were opening up in some areas, even as in others the fight was being conducted to maintain some small semblance of hope amidst mass unemployment.

One thing which was general, however, was the indifference of central government to the suffering of the working class, and the antipathy of owners and management to any exercise of trade union power. Jack Jones recalls:

management tended to regard attempts at organising for the trade unions as an interference with their business ... for example, the negotiation of piece work prices was not regarded as one in which the union had any role, the employer thought they were the sole body to determine what should be paid to work people … the idea of conciliation and negotiation was not in their minds.[16]

The union was forthright in blaming the capitalist system for the mass unemployment that remained an abiding feature of the 1930s: 'Capitalism continually aims at beating wages to a lower level, and the more it succeeds the worse it fails as a system', said Irish regional chairman C. O'Rourke in the April 1936 issue of the *T&G Record*:

Low wages prevent the workers from buying the goods they produce, and thus, for want of purchases, the markets are glutted, demand ceases, production falls off – you have unemployment and trade depression. The capitalist class have never been able to perceive these plain facts. All they think of is grab, grab.

Bevin contests Gateshead for Labour in 1931 (unsuccessfully)

The national coalition government increased means testing, in order to cut unemployment assistance to bare subsistence levels. This was condemned as 'wretched meanness' by Bevin. Medical revelations about the growth of malnutrition had stirred the nation, he said:

> Yet here we are, one of the wealthiest countries in the world, with well fed men and women sitting in the government, in parliament and in the treasury, cogitating, examining and manipulating the scales, to ascertain the lowest possible point to which they can go to save themselves from being accused of starving the people.[17]

Bevin called on the labour movement to fight for a better standard and not to rest until it was secured – and these were not just words. The T&G was fully involved in the mass campaign in South Wales to resist reductions in the rate of unemployment benefit, which forced the National government to back down and restore the cuts.

Bevin had started to develop his ideas for a positive economic programme even earlier, while the second Labour government was still clinging to office:

> Private enterprise having proved totally unable to lift the country out of the morass in which it is, there seems no alternative but for the state to grapple with the problem and for large measures of state planning to be adopted.

He also produced a pamphlet arguing for measures to cut the dole queues. *My Plan for 2,000,000 Workers* advocated a state pension to encourage workers to retire; an optional pension at 60; invalidity benefits for the war wounded; raising the school leaving age to 16; and a forty-hour working week – all proposals designed to create new demand for labour.[18]

Alongside addressing the big picture, the union had to deal with pressing industrial concerns among its own membership. The casualisation of docks labour persisted in the 1930s, even though there had been some measures of improvement. The Port of London Authority had a register of dockers, but because there were more registered dockers than work available for most of the time, this did not end the brutal struggle to secure employment. Alex Gander, a London docker, remembers: 'we were like animals in the struggle to get close to the foreman and catch his eye ... That would lead to aggro, sometimes fights'. Some dockers pretended to be Irish in order to win favour with foremen from that country, even wearing green scarves for effect![19]

If employer resistance was the main obstacle to decasualisation, divisions in the docks workforce itself did not make the union's job any easier. Some dockers enjoyed the relative freedom which casual labour gave them, allowing them to work or not as they pleased. This was the issue that led to the defection of the Glasgow Docks branch. It declared itself against decasualisation, which it saw as an 'instrument of discipline and coercion', and as something being pushed by officials who were only interested in stabilising membership, in order to provide themselves 'with the maximum security in the undisturbed enjoyment of their salaries and superannuations'. On this issue and the related demand for the election of their full-time officials, the Glasgow dockers broke away, setting up the Scottish Transport and General Workers Union, which remained in existence down to the 1970s. Such local and particular difficulties are an inevitable part of the life of a general trade union, however vexing the central leadership sometimes found them. Bevin was particularly put out when the tinplate men of South Wales rejected a pension scheme that the general secretary had spent years negotiating, and which the employers had finally accepted.[20]

During this period the union made progress in road transport, its other traditional stronghold. We look at the special case of the London Buses below, but the T&G's efforts were not confined either to the capital or to the passenger sector. In 1935 it sustained a twelve-week strike by Dublin tramwaymen, and Bevin made major

Bevin presents a compensation cheque secured for a member. Such legal support was a vital part of the T&G's work.

progress in establishing national standards in the road haulage industry, including on wages and the regulation of small carriers; these were embodied in the Road Haulage Wages Act of 1938. The union organised a major drive to expand the Road Transport Commercial trade group, in order to help ensure that these new laws were observed in an industry by then employing well over one million workers. Resources were also committed to the organisation of the passenger industry outside London. Inside London, the passenger section was a story in itself.

On the London Buses

According to Bullock, in the 1930s the union's London Bus section 'took the place of the Docks Group ... as the storm centre of the Union'. The section embraced 20,000 highly organised workers, with a strong tradition of industrial autonomy and a large degree of latitude within the union's structure. Leadership within the section increasingly devolved onto a rank-and-file movement that often ran ahead of the official structures in organising strike action over pay, hours and conditions – designed to enhance their perceived status as an industrial elite. As a well organised group concentrated in large garages across a relatively small area, they were well placed to develop such a strategy, as their historian Ken Fuller (himself much later an officer of the union) outlines in his outstanding work on this section. Their aggressive policy had a broad following among the men – in Fuller's words, they considered themselves to be '"aristocrats" of the whole working class'. This policy did not, however, commend itself to Bevin.[21]

The bus workers' agitation was inevitably denounced by the press as the work of Communists, even before the Communist Party had started to involve itself in the bus workers' rank-and-file movement. Increasingly, such opinions chimed with Bevin's own. The general secretary's anti-Communism was fuelled not only by his developing 'social partnership' outlook, but also by his great distaste for and distrust of any unofficial movement outside of the union's constitutional structures – and his own control. This collision of attitudes shaped relations between Bevin and the London Bus section throughout the 1930s.[22]

The lead within the section was taken by a group of militants, of whom Bert Papworth and Bill Jones became the most celebrated. Papworth had led his first strikes during the first world war at the age of 16, and had been involved in disputes at the Woolwich Arsenal. He and Jones both joined the Communist Party during the 1930s.

The 1937 Coronation strike – so called because it coincided with the coronation of George VI – was effectively headed by their rank-and-file committee, although it was an official strike. Twenty-five thousand bus workers went out for a reduction in the onerous rotas and hours to which they were subjected. Bevin backed the action in the face of a media manufactured outcry (because it coincided with the royal event), and led the presentation of the men's case at the hastily-established court of inquiry with his usual diligence, a fact acknowledged by Papworth. Despite this, an antipathy existed between the section members and the leadership, which was only increased when the men turned down the deal that Bevin had negotiated. After a pause that was designed to undermine the rank-and-file leadership and highlight its inability to secure a settlement, the strikers found themselves ordered back to work by the general secretary (with Executive backing), on the same terms as had already been on offer.[23]

As a consequence of the 'Coronation strike', Bevin decided to effectively outlaw unofficial movements amongst the membership. The London lead had been taken up by busworkers in many other parts of the country, leading to disputes which the General Executive Council had refused to recognise, and exacerbating the problem. An internal inquiry urged that 'a definite end ... be put to rank and file and similar organisations within the union, or any other form of organisation not authorised by the constitution'. This included a ban on issuing unauthorised journals and literature and circulating model resolutions. Papworth and Jones were expelled from the union, although they were readmitted before very long. Later both became members of the T&G executive and, in Papworth's case, the TUC General Council. The decisions on rank-and-file activity were vigorously opposed by the Central Bus Committee, all the members of which resigned at one point in protest. Most did not break away from the union however. While a split was initiated by some of those disgusted with Bevin and the central leadership of the union, this was vigorously opposed by the Communist Party – 'disunity on our part means strength for the Board' – and it fizzled out after a few years.[24]

Building the organisation

In 1937 the T&G surpassed the miners' union to become the largest trade union in Great Britain, a distinction it held until the creation of Unison in the 1990s (which resulted from the amalgamation of three public sector unions) and regained in 2007 with the merger to form Unite. The union enjoyed four years of double-digit percentage growth in membership from 1932, as the economy recovered somewhat from the slump and new industries were developed, particularly in and around London. This upward trend even survived a bold decision by Bevin to lapse 40,000 non-paying members in 1932, more than ten per cent of the total at the time.[25]

The expansion in membership was led by the new Metal, Engineering and Chemical trade group which, building largely on the Workers' Union inheritance, gave the T&G a strong position in the engineering and car industries. The group had overtaken the Docks group in membership size before the end of the decade. It also gave the union a more balanced geographical profile, with the new membership concentrated in the Midlands, London and the South-East.

The case for getting organised

Building the union in the newer industries was not much easier than it had been in the docks two generations earlier, at least from the point of view of the necessity of confronting entrenched management hostility. The Pressed Steel strike in Oxford in 1934 is an example. This plant, ancillary to the Morris motor works there, had a large semi-skilled workforce, with many former Welsh miners (heirs to their own militant trade union tradition) among them.

> The factory lines were often speeded up to meet deadlines, and workers who were too slow dismissed. No formal tea or lavatory breaks were allowed. The noise was nerve shattering … No proper canteens existed and food had to be consumed on the factory floor. Other personal injuries as well as loss of hearing, included asbestosis, loss of fingers, bits of metal flying at high speed into eyes, lead poisoning and death.[26]

Unsurprisingly, these conditions led to rebellion. Perhaps more surprisingly it was women workers who led the struggle (the initial impetus coming from the local branch of the Communist Party), organising a demonstration right through the factory after management declined to meet them to discuss their pay. The T&G backed the strike over pay and union recognition, though it was declared unconstitutional by the established unions in the industry, the AEU and the National Union of Vehicle Builders. The T&G also paid strike benefit in the dispute, even though most of the workers were technically not entitled to it as they were very recent union recruits. Nationwide solidarity was organised, both through the T&G and other unions (including railway workers in Swindon), while workers at the largely unorganised Morris plant threatened action if their management tried to break the Pressed Steel strike. Their subsequent victory established the T&G's first position in the motor industry; and it proved that – in the big factories as in the docks – semi-skilled workers could be organised: trade unionism need not be the preserve of a craft elite. It also led to a wave of unionisation throughout other industries in Oxford and the surrounding county. Management at Pressed Steel counter-attacked from time to time throughout the decade, including dismissing the convenor for 'insubordination', but by the end of the 1930s the union had a strong shop stewards network, mainly based on young men originally from Wales and Scotland.[27]

There was growth elsewhere too. A merger in 1934 with the 'Altogether' Builders' Labourers and Constructional Workers Society led to a much stronger organisation in the construction industry. And new sections were established within the General Workers trade group for agriculture, central and local government, flour milling and fisheries. Even stable lads found a place in the expanding T&G, with the union giving full support to a long strike at Lambourn stables in Berkshire.

Just as significant for the future, the T&G's overwhelmingly masculine profile started to alter. The move into lighter industries, away from the old port regions, created both the opportunity and the necessity for the greater recruitment of women workers. 'The Girls Are Game – Are You?' read a placard held by the women workers on strike at Pressed Steel in 1934, the call to solidarity allied to a probably intentional sexual challenge. As new domestic goods industries sprung up across the Midlands and around London, women workers began to self-organise and then to flock towards the T&G, if for no other reason than that the AEU refused to admit them. The Lucas 'girls strike' in Birmingham in 1931 was a significant example. At Courtaulds, management hastened to call in the T&G rather than negotiate with the stroppy female rank-and-file.

Mary Quaile and Mary Carlin were the first women's officers of the union and, as Tony Topham records:

> these two undertook the unspectacular and grinding task of factory-gate recruitment of women workers, at a time when an enrolment of a few dozen here and a handful there was reported

A strike at Siemens in 1939

with relief and pleasure. They were the reward for the influenza, bronchitis and colds which those two often suffered after a stint in freezing or rain-soaked conditions.[28]

Often women were too frightened to join the union, but not all their problems were external to the T&G. Patronising attitudes were rife within: 'Bring your women-folk along and enrol them as members at once' the early *Record* encouraged its male readership. There was also strong resistance to the introduction of female labour into some parts of the workforce, for example in the passenger transport industry.[29]

By 1937 the T&G boasted 654,510 members, more than any other union in the world (outside the USSR). And it was already a very different, more diverse union than that of 1922. Much of its work was modernised, with the development of an extensive education service, and new resources being allocated to the research department at Central Office.[30]

It was at the very centre of the labour movement in Britain. Bevin had early on determined that the union should have a building which befitted its status, and had invested a great deal of time and money in the establishment of Transport House as the union's Central Office in Smith Square, London, within a stone's throw of the Houses of Parliament and government offices. The TUC, the Labour Party and the International Transport Workers Federation all took space in the building for their own headquarters. As a result, for generations the words 'Transport House' became virtually synonymous with the labour movement's national leadership. The TUC remained a T&G tenant until the 1950s and the Labour Party into the 1980s. (This impressive and historic building was eventually sold by the union in 1994, a generally unpopular decision.)

Among other contributions, Bevin led a successful struggle throughout the decade to save the newspaper the *Daily Herald* as the daily voice of the labour movement. The paper was to remain in business for a further thirty years, before eventually being transformed into Rupert Murdoch's *Sun*. Bevin had grasped, perhaps more clearly than anyone else in the movement, the importance of a Labour daily at a time when the rest of the national press was hostile.[31]

Two historic figures, Gosling and Tillett, had retired at the start of the decade, still further enhancing Bevin's pre-eminence. With Gosling's departure the post of full-time President was abandoned, and for the rest of the T&G's existence the General Executive Council was headed by a lay Chair. The first was Herbert Kershaw, a tram driver from Bradford. There was change too among the senior full-time officers, with John Cliff resigning as assistant general secretary in 1932 to join the newly created London Passenger Transport Board. 'As right wing as Bevin, but a capable man', in the view of Bill Jones, Cliff was not initially replaced. A few years later, the number two post was taken up by Arthur Deakin, about whom much more later.[32]

The union's undoubted achievements, and the benefits that working people gained from them in the very difficult decade of the 1930s, should not blind us to the faults of the T&G at the time. In particular, there was a continuing tension between the union's democratic structures and Bevin's authoritarian leadership – his handling of the London Bus membership was far from unusual. Jack Jones, who joined the union in the Liverpool docks in the 1930s, recalls an unofficial overtime ban on Salford docks: 'At Bevin's instigation, the three leaders of the ban were expelled from the union and lost their employment. It was an example of his ruthlessness. He brooked no opposition.'[33]

And there was a still more fundamental tension – between the T&G's essence as an organisation representing working-class interests and the pull of class collaboration, particularly strong after the defeat of 1926. Jones again: 'Full-time trade union officials on the docks were inclined to become tin-pot dictators, supporting the decisions of management and resenting any queries or complaints

The founder at his desk

from the men'. And later, 'the union in the Liverpool area ... had become a disciplinary arm acting on behalf of the employer.' As for Bevin, 'there were times when some of us felt he was responding to the overtures of big business and the establishment rather more than was good for the union'. However Jones, like almost all the internal critics, was nevertheless 'immensely impressed by Bevin as a negotiator'.[34]

No doubt these experiences helped cement Jones's own commitment to decentralised, member-led democracy thirty years later, but in the 1930s 'to speak your mind in the union was like walking on glass'.[35]

Resisting fascism

As the decade unwound, the need to resist the rise of fascism both in Britain and across Europe came to dominate the preoccupations of the labour movement. This was a struggle fought out on several fronts – against pacifism within the Labour Party, against appeasement of dictators by the Tory leaders, against the home-grown Mosley fascists on the streets and, most significantly in terms of immediate human cost, against the Franco rising in Spain from 1936 onwards.

Fascism was rooted in the crisis which had swept Europe in the years after the First World War, years which had completely dislocated class relations and seen a vast increase in working-class opposition to capitalism. In many countries this had led to the point of revolution – a danger to which the ruling-class response was often to impose a right-wing dictatorship. Mussolini's Italy, in which left-wing political parties were banned and trade unions incorporated into the state apparatus, provided the template. But it was Hitler's accession to power in Germany in 1933 which turned the rise of fascism into a continent-wide crisis. The Nazi leader not only added a rabid anti-semitism to fascism's ideological mix, he also sought a sweeping rearrangement in the European balance of power in favour of Germany – a rearrangement which could only be secured by the war which Hitler actively looked forward to.

In Britain fascism had its supporters, most notably *Daily Mail* proprietor Viscount Rothermere and former Labour MP Oswald Mosley, although they never amounted to more than a minority of the establishment, which in general found the methods of the 'National' government sufficient for its requirements. Far wider ruling-class circles, while not looking to Hitlerite methods at home, were quite ready to appease the German dictator's foreign policy demands, in the hope that war might either be averted or – perhaps better still – waged by Germany against the Soviet Union.

Labour had its own problems in facing up to fascism. Pacifist sentiment was strong, in the aftermath of the slaughter in the trenches, and there was a widespread reluctance to advocate rearmament while such a move meant placing more weapons in the hands of the distrusted National government. Bevin was among the first to grasp the nettle of the new international situation, denouncing fascism right from the start, and pressing for support for rearmament to confront it.

However, the T&G leader was not yet sure-footed in the political arena. In the words of one historian, 'Bevin believed that working-class power lay in the trade unions and not in the Labour Party', and, while he was inevitably drawn into Labour Party business, as for example in 1931, because of his stature among the trade unions, he was at this stage insensitive to some of the requirements of political diplomacy, and too inclined to conduct party business in the same robust way as had worked for him in the T&G.[36]

It was in this context that Bevin made his celebrated attack on George Lansbury, then Labour's leader, at the 1935 party conference. Determined to force Labour to abandon those pacifist attitudes which undermined resistance to fascism, and of which Lansbury was the most consistent and popular exponent, he denounced the revered leader for 'taking your conscience round from body to body asking to be told what you ought to do with it'.

The speech was received very badly in the hall, but Bevin's policy point was carried. Unrepentant, he justified his denunciation of the party's icon: 'Lansbury has been going about in saint's cloths for years, waiting for martyrdom. I set fire to the faggots'.[37]

The intervention was an historic one, since it forced Lansbury's departure from the party leadership in the run-up to the 1935 General Election, to be replaced by Clement Attlee, one of the few Labour MPs who had survived the 1931 electoral massacre and who was later, of course, to become Labour's most successful Prime Minister.

But Bevin was not as decisive in all aspects of resistance to fascism. Under his guidance, the T&G blocked any suggestion of a united front against the rising danger. Thus, when the time came to block the Mosleyites from marching through Jewish districts of London's East End, it was to the Communists that dockers looked for a lead. Nor was the Bevin of the 1930s a follower of the Bevin of 1920 who had strongly advocated the use of industrial muscle to force a change in government foreign policy. He spoke out against the use of the strike weapon to oppose war at Labour's conference in 1934, and later opposed any use of strikes to force an end to appeasement or in support for the beleaguered Spanish Republic. It was probably true that such a call would not have received a sufficiently strong echo in a movement still licking the wounds of 1926. However, it remains the case that Bevin was an advocate of a strong stand by the British state against fascism, but not of direct working-class action to oppose it, either at home or in Spain.[38]

Bevin's contradictory attitude towards resisting fascism was caught in an interview with Jack Jones when the latter was on his way over to Spain to serve in the International Brigades that had been mobilised to offer armed solidarity to the democratic government. He started by questioning Jones's motives – 'have the Communists been after you?' – before acknowledging that resisting fascism was more than just a Communist preoccupation, and adding: 'Britain must stand up to these dictators, but we need to be stronger.'[39] Jones, who was wounded in the course of his service in Spain, later took the view that 'Bevin regarded the Spanish situation as nothing to do with us ... he saw [that] the effort to try to support the Spanish people had come from the left and he regarded that as suspect.'

Jones was not, of course, the only T&G member to fight in Spain. Take the case of Dalston bus branch member Bill Brisky. Bill Jones, one of the leaders of the London Bus section, reported that when Brisky volunteered to join the International Brigades he had left one of his most treasured possessions with his union colleagues for safe keeping: 'Should the nazis take him prisoner they will not find Bill Brisky's trade union card; we have that, keeping our promise ... to keep it clear.'

Like so many trade unionists in the Spanish struggle, Bill Brisky made the ultimate sacrifice for democracy, dying in the defence of Madrid. Writing his obituary, Bill Jones turned his martyrdom against Bevin:

> Bill's death has many lessons for us all – for none more than his General Secretary with his fat well-fed belly (made possible by the Bill Briskys of the working class), afraid of fascism, as he is afraid of the whole boss class, knowing only two words: *unofficial* and *reds*, who ... sent the Spanish trade union leaders back home convinced that they can expect no real help from the Citrines and Bevins, knowing that they must depend on the Bill Briskys who only have their lives to offer.[41]

Bill Jones's strictures may seem unnecessarily harsh. Nevertheless, while posterity (and this work, for that matter) will inevitably dwell more on the role of the Bevins, the T&G story is in its essentials the story of the Briskys.

Notes

1. Bullock, p213.
2. Bullock, p246.
3. *British Worker*, 6 May 1926.

4. Fuller, p93, citing Allen Hutt.
5. Bullock, p337.
6. Bullock, p353.
7. Williams, pp401-2.
8. Williams, p403.
9. Bullock, p374.
10. Bullock, p221; Allen p49.
11. Hyman, p8.
12. Coates/Topham, p773.
13. Hyman, pp160ff.
14. Hyman, ibid.
15. Coates/Topham, 2, p18.
16. Geoffrey Goodman interview.
17. *T&G Record*, July 1936.
18. Bullock, pp433, 516.
19. Weightman etc, p215.
20. Bullock, pp467, 605.
21. Bullock, p519; Fuller p71.
22. Fuller, pp100ff.
23. Allen, p66; Bullock, p608 ff; Fuller, pp144ff.
24. Allen, pp69-70; Fuller, p161; Bullock, p613.
25. Bullock, p525.
26. 5/625 anniversary pamphlet, p6.
27. Croucher, pp28ff.
28. Coates/Topham 2, p34.
29. Coates/Topham 2, p36.
30. Bullock p 620;
31. Bullock, p 419.
32. Bullock, p455; Fuller, p134.
33. Jones, p33.
34. Jones, p29, pp82-83.
35. Jones, p35.
36. Allen, p86.
37. Pimlott, p73.
38. Allen, p87.
39. Jones, p61.
40. Geoffrey Goodman interview.
41. Fuller, p127.

3. The T&G at war 1939-1945

The outbreak of war in 1939 was the inevitable consequence of the failure of the western powers to stand up to escalating fascist aggression throughout the decade. The German invasion of Poland finally made conflict unavoidable, although that did not stop the British and French governments from continuing to endeavour to avoid it.

September 1939 marked, in fact, less the start of a fighting war in the west than the start of a 'phoney war' in which neither side did much of anything. In the case of official Britain and France, this reflected their eternal hope that the conflict could still be deflected eastwards, towards the Soviet Union, despite its non-aggression pact with Germany. This 'phoney' period did not come to an end until the Nazis attacked in the west in May 1940.

The labour movement, in its great majority, supported the war from the outset as a long-overdue stand against fascism. It did not however, support the 'war effort' because, at that stage, there wasn't one. Britain continued to be ruled by the 'National' (read Tory) government of Neville Chamberlain, as concerned with the maintenance of class privilege as opposition to Hitler. Labour remained in parliamentary opposition.

Ernie Bevin put it clearly in October 1939:

> The principle of equality has not yet been won – equality not merely in the economic sense but in conception and in the attitude of mind of those in power. We do not desire to serve on any

committee or body as an act of patronage. We represent probably
the most vital factor in the state: without our people the war
cannot be won nor can the life of the country be carried on. The
assumption that the only brains in the country are in the heads of
the Federation of British Industries and Big Business has yet to be
corrected.[1]

This assumption was later to be corrected by Bevin in person.

Under these circumstances, the T&G and the rest of the
movement kept its powder dry, unwilling to make unilateral
concessions to a narrow class-based government, and one which,
moreover, bore a large measure of responsibility for the war, thanks
to the failures of its foreign policy. Bevin was highly suspicious of
Chamberlain's attempt to bring the unions into state administration
in some subordinate capacity, and of talk of emergency powers for
government. He told the T&G GEC in March 1940: 'the thing we
have to do is to maintain our union intact and to be ready to fight
for liberty immediately it is challenged'.[2]

The Tories claimed to want to involve industry in putting the
economy on a war footing but, as Alan Bullock pointed out
'industry to the Chamberlain government meant capital and
management, not labour'. In his last major speech as the T&G's
leader, on May Day 1940, Ernie Bevin outlined what was the
mainstream trade union view of the prevailing crisis: 'The British
working class want this war won. They know what is at stake. It is
their liberty. But they want a government that is going to please the
nation before its friends and private interests'. Here he was
referring to the capitalists already securing bigger profits as a result
of the war.[3]

Bevin leaves his union

The Second World War, and the trade union approach to it, changed
just a few days later. In spring 1940 Hitler's armies began their

western aggression, over-running first Denmark and Norway, then Belgium and Holland and ultimately France. This precipitated the final crisis of confidence in the Chamberlain government and its ability to prosecute the war effectively. The Tories at last realised the need for a real coalition to govern a Britain now faced with the menace of imminent invasion, but the Labour Party made it clear that it could not serve under the government's existing leadership. In the face of the gravest-ever threat to Britain's independent sovereign existence, Winston Churchill – an arch-opponent of appeasement (if not always fascism), and the union's enemy in 1926 – now became Prime Minister.

The Labour Party thereupon agreed to enter office for the first time since 1931, as part of an administration that could at last be described as genuinely 'national'. Bevin fully backed that approach, but he does not seem to have expected what followed – an invitation for him to take up membership in the inner 'war cabinet'. Attlee, acting for Churchill, asked the T&G leader to become the new Minister of Labour, responsible for mobilising what would now doubtless be termed the country's 'human resources' for war.

Bevin accepted office with little apparent hesitation. Some colleagues believed that he should have held out for a more senior office, such as the Ministry of Munitions, but they little realised what Bevin would make of the Ministry of Labour. Bevin himself took the view that this was scarcely the moment for haggling over portfolios. His only reservation lay in his determination not to proceed without the sanction of the T&G's lay leadership, although it was scarcely credible that it would have been refused. Bevin told the GEC: 'This is the most difficult part of all. I may never come back. Well, brothers, if I do not – you cannot tell how long the war will last – I really hate leaving the Union, but duty calls and I respond.'[4]

And with that he was gone. Although Bevin's role as Minister of Labour, and to a smaller degree his subsequent job as Foreign

Secretary, had an impact on the life of the union, from May 1940 onwards the history of the T&G and that of its architect are largely different stories. Bevin did not formally lay down his office of General Secretary for a further five years; Arthur Deakin was appointed 'acting General Secretary', with consequential adjustments further down the hierarchy. But Bevin played little further direct part in the work of the T&G. He attended the Biennial Delegate Conferences of 1941 and 1943, but went to no meetings of the GEC until the end of 1944. Until the end of his life he kept closely in touch with the T&G, doubtless to Deakin's irritation, but it was no longer Bevin's union.[5]

Face-to-face with dockers

This may be the moment then to consider Bevin's reputation and industrial legacy, as the T&G moved on to life without him and he himself embraced fresh challenges. Perhaps more than any other leader of the T&G, Bevin stands out as a complex and contradictory figure, who cannot be summarised in the few swift and clear phrases with which one could characterise an Arthur Deakin or a Jack Jones.

He was, on the one hand, a right-winger in the terms of the movement of his era, and he became more so as time passed. While his subsequent performance as Foreign Secretary should not colour any judgement on his record as T&G leader, there is no doubt that even in 1940 Bevin was well on the way to becoming part of the establishment. Unlike many of his peers in the movement leadership however (then and since), there is little evidence that he saw this as a question of personal advancement – rather it was a mark of labour coming into its proper role as an estate of the realm, to be treated on an equal footing with the upper classes.

That advance to securing for the working class its proper place in the nation had been the hallmark of his approach and outlook. Certainly since 1926, if not earlier, he had not sought the end of capitalism, except perhaps through the most gradual process of reform. He was a negotiator and an organiser, but not a revolutionary. For him the measures of working-class advance were the growth in the organised strength of the T&G and the trade unions as a whole, and the degree to which their concerns were acted upon, together with their success in overcoming class prejudice and becoming integrated into the nation's life at the highest level.

Bevin was also undoubtedly an autocrat. In the words of one left-wing historian, he 'enjoyed power blatantly and ruled his union despotically'. J.T. Murphy, by then an independent left-winger, summarised Bevin thus: 'He believes that Socialism comes through the more efficient organisation of capitalism and the increasing power of organised labour ... He is a great organiser and as ruthless as Stalin with his opponents.'[6]

These judgements may seem on the harsh side, particularly that of Murphy. Bevin undoubtedly set out in the belief that the concentration of power in the office of the General Secretary was essential to the T&G's survival as a power in industry, and he subsequently came to believe in it as an end in itself. He devoted himself to dominating most aspects of the union's life long after its continued existence was no longer in question. But at the same time, he had to lead by persuasion. While he was not averse to the application of disciplinary sanction against critics who overstepped what he saw as the mark, at every stage in policy and organisation he had to carry a majority of the union's lay leadership with him. And his life as T&G leader often seems like a long argument with his members on one issue after another, which is not the way of unchallenged despots. Nevertheless, he did increasingly come to see criticism as disloyalty, and when this came from Communists or other organised left-wingers, his authoritarian and right-wing attitudes fused into an unpleasant mixture which, while by no means reaching the levels of Arthur Deakin's post-war McCarthyism, certainly pre-figured it. It is no surprise that left-wing critics saw Bevin, by the time of World War Two, as a pillar of the capitalist order rather than an opponent of it.

Yet if the T&G was his monument, then Bevin's legacy is secure. He left the union as the strongest working-class organisation in the capitalist world, increasingly entrenched in growing and dynamic areas of the industrial economy, and with a flexible structure that endured unmodified after him, taking trade unionism out to a mass of workers who would certainly have otherwise remained unorganised and super-exploited. The T&G had undoubtedly already secured real and significant improvements in working and social conditions for its membership, and had become a dominant voice in the counsels of the TUC and the Labour Party. And despite the observations above, it never ceased to operate on the basis of a democratic constitution, which ultimately afforded the membership the decisive say in the formulation of policy.

Wartime changes

Bevin's brief as Minister of Labour included coordinating the drive to increase industrial production. This was essential if the economy was to be mobilised for victory, and Bevin saw the main problem as lying in myopic and profit-driven management, which had failed to utilise the latent human potential in their factories. He sought and got the powers to address this situation. Indeed, he enjoyed greater powers than any other minister in Churchill's cabinet, and great influence over the Prime Minister himself.

The new Minister of Labour had 'the control and use of all labour', being empowered to 'direct any person in the United Kingdom to perform any such services as he might specify'; he could compel employers to keep records, and had the power 'to make orders for regulating the engagement of workers by employers and the duration of their employment'. He also had the necessary credibility to ask his trade union comrades for the relaxation of union regulations in vital industries.[7]

This led to the involvement of workers in planning and organising production for the first time in Britain's industrial history, through Joint Production Committees set up by the government. These worked to boost output while entrenching union and workers' rights. Bevin also used his new bully pulpit to urge all workers to join their appropriate trade union, as a sort of patriotic duty in the cause of organised production, something that no doubt contributed to the very rapid war-time growth in trade union membership.

A joint consultative committee of the Ministry of Labour – representing unions, employers and government – was set up to agree all proposals to meet the requirements of war-time production prior to their introduction. And a number of specific measures were implemented, one of which, the establishment of a National Dock Labour Corporation in June 1941, had a great and immediate impact on the T&G's membership.

Bevin and Deakin were both deeply involved in this major attack on the perennial problem of casualisation. All dockers were brought within the Essential Work Order with the creation of the Corporation. As Deakin commented, the scheme might last only for the duration of the war, but 'setting up as it does a form of workers' control, expressed through the trade union organisations acting jointly with representative employers, it may be regarded as a great experiment – the principle of which we may desire to retain'.[8]

The Essential Works Orders departed radically from the pre-war *laissez-faire* dogma. They covered 8.5 million workers and made it illegal, *inter alia*, for any employer to dismiss a worker without authority of the Ministry, a move about which Bevin informed members of the union in the January 1941 *T&G Record*. The orders also made strikes illegal, but this provision was scarcely used after resistance by Kent miners had proved it could not be effective against even a moderately large group of workers. If there were very few strikes in the early years of the war, this was largely a consequence of support for the war effort among the working class, support certainly encouraged by union officials. As Bevin said on a visit to the Midlands, 'the trade unions are fighting for the country and every factory is part of the battlefront'. Strikes did increase as the war continued, however, when defeat by the Nazis began to seem unlikely and economic frustrations mounted.[9]

The entry of the Soviet Union into the war in June 1941 certainly enhanced commitment to the anti-Hitler cause in the factories, docks and depots. Alan Hutt observed that after the Soviet entry into the war the unions began acting more purposefully in many vital factories, to boost production and deal with waste, bungling and chaos. The London bus workers' journal *The Transporter* expressed views widely held at the time:

Nothing about this war is the same as it was before Germany's attack on Soviet Russia. Not only has a bigger force than ever before been drawn into the struggle, but a force of *an entirely different kind* [emphasis in original]. Hitler is now fighting the only people in the world without capitalists. He is fighting the largest body of organised trade unionists in the world – trade unionists who run and own the industries they work in.

Even Bevin abandoned his anticommunism for a time, saying that 'nothing gave me greater joy than when … the Cabinet decided to accept the twenty years' treaty with Russia', and he compared the USSR's struggle for global recognition with the similar advances of his own labour movement.[10]

But it was far from all being sunshine on the industrial front. The most obvious problem was the physical danger from the Luftwaffe's bombing of industrial areas. Not only was this a menace to life and limb, it also had the side-effect of disrupting trade union life, since meetings became difficult to organise and those union activists who were not mobilised in the forces often wished to be at home with their families when not at work, in case the bombers came over that night.

And there was still the problem of recalcitrant and hostile management who 'didn't know there was a war on'. Jack Jones, a newly-appointed T&G officer in Coventry, a city with scores of vital engineering and armament factories, recalls: 'Management continued to give no quarter, trade unions were still regarded as an "alien force". What we were doing was challenging the divine right of management, and they didn't like it.' He even recalls the owner of one machine tool company waving a revolver at him and threatening the use of the Official Secrets Act for the impertinence of trying to organise his firm.[11]

But the times were changing. According to Jones:

the early 1940s in the Coventry area saw a remarkable transformation in attitudes on the shop floor. At the start managements had done everything possible to prevent people from recruiting for the unions … Step by step we inched forward until it became commonplace for shop stewards to be elected at shop-floor meetings, to hold committee meetings during working hours, and to report back, after meetings with management or the works committee, to members on the shop floor.[12]

Women and shop stewards

In the course of the war Arthur Deakin made what must have sounded like a sensational statement to a T&G meeting. 'Women,' he said, 'are here to stay'. This was indeed one of the most important transformations in the T&G and the unions more generally during the war. As during the 1914-1918 conflict, the absence of men in the armed forces meant huge numbers of women workers were drafted into the factories and exposed to the rigours and rhythms of industrial life. But this time they were encouraged to join unions that were (relatively) welcoming. The Miss Price who lost her fingers in an accident at Gloster Aircraft in 1942, and for whom T&G was able to secure £4,000 in compensation, would not have had such support in the First World War.[13]

As a result of this changed environment and its own organising

Women in the factories

efforts, the T&G recorded a ninefold increase in female membership during the war, reaching a total of 306,707 by the end of 1943. The craft engineering and electrical unions even admitted women to membership for the first time.[14]

In 1943 the T&G organised its first-ever women's conference, the agenda of which included the need for more nurseries, the eligibility of the children of part-time workers to attend such nurseries, clinics, and communal feeding centres. Progress on some of these demands was expedited by a government keen to tackle the problem of absenteeism in the factories, which, unsurprisingly, was much higher among women with child-care and other caring responsibilities.[15]

Employers were often unenthusiastic about acting on such demands. As women's labour was brought into a range of industries, equal pay was agreed in some cases (such as for bus workers), but not in others. In the words of T&G-sponsored Labour MP Jennie Adamson of Dartford, 'many employers were exploiting the patriotism of the women by paying them low wages and enforcing long hours'. Adamson went on to call for action to stamp out this exploitation of the war-time spirit.

The union itself was slow to change – most shop stewards were men and, as Jack Jones noted, they did not always support women's demands. But the T&G's record was still one to be proud of. In 1942 the T&G asked the engineering employers federation for an agreement for part-time workers, who had received no increase under the national agreement. Other unions supported this initiative but, as one historian noted, it was the TGWU that had started the ball rolling, 'as in so many matters affecting women'.[16]

Overall, T&G membership surpassed the one million mark in the course of the war. The increase was general across all trade groups but was particularly enormous in the Metal, Engineering and Chemical group, which rose from just 100,000 in 1938 to over 400,000 by 1942. Major gains were made in the Midlands and in the aircraft industry – in Coventry, membership rose from under 2,000 to 20,000, thanks to organising efforts led by Jack Jones and others.[17]

The Transport and General Workers' Union

WILL HOLD

A GREAT

OPEN-AIR RALLY

On SATURDAY, JUNE 6th, 1942, at 6.30 p.m.,
At The White Hart Hotel Yard, Dunmow.

Bro. A. S. PARSONSON, Secretary, Dunmow Branch, will preside.

SPEAKERS :

Organiser A. EDWARDS
Member Essex Agricultural Wages Committee.

Divisional Organiser JACK SHINGFIELD
Leader of Workers' Side, Essex Agricultural Wages Committee ; Leader of Workers' Side,
Suffolk Agricultural Wages Committee ; and Member of the National Agricultural Wages Board.

Every Farm Worker in the district is invited to come along and support
OLD FRIENDS. Old Friends who have proved their worth **TO YOU**

LOOK AT THE RESULTS :

1914: Farm workers' wages, 15/- a week. Hours—dawn to dark. No overtime pay, no holidays, no half-day, no unemployment pay.

1942: Minimum wage, £3 for 48 hours in winter, 50 hours in summer; proper half-day holidays, overtime, and unemployment benefit.

The Farm Worker who joins this Union is assured of the support of its 1,000,000 members.

UNITY IS STRENGTH

Do you remember what happened to Farm Workers' wages in 1921 ?

Did they fall from 46/6 to 27/- per week ? **YOU KNOW!**

What will happen when the war ends ? **YOU DON'T KNOW!!**

JOIN THIS UNION NOW AND MAKE CERTAIN OF ITS PROTECTION

The Essex County Telegraph, Head Street, Colchester.

Organising in the countryside during the war

This great change in the quantity of trade unionists led to a change in the quality of trade unionism. In the words of historian Angus Calder in his book *The People's War*:

Such expansion made it harder than ever for the bureaucracies to exercise control over unruly elements. Former officials were now in the forces and had been replaced by inexperienced recruits … The gulf between leaders and rank-and-file yawned wider than ever. The procedure for settlement of disputes slowed down until it seemed to impatient new recruits that they were halting altogether … The shop steward stepped into the breach, as the elected representative of the workpeople who could air and settle problems on the spot … The shop steward now became the key man in maintaining the union's hold over its members …[18]

This may have made some full-time officials uneasy. But it marked the start of the shift of power in trade unions downwards – something which Arthur Deakin later opposed with might and main, but which, still later, Jack Jones became the evangelist for.

Certainly, the T&G brought a different attitude to trade unionism in the factories. Harold Taylor, a T&G official at Armstrong-Whitworth Aircraft, painted this picture:

> There was a couple of the old AEU stewards ... they were still doffing their caps at the boss, and we had started not to doff our caps. We were demanding seats when they called us in to give us some information or tell us something, we were able to say 'Well, are we going to stand here all bloody day, or are you going to give us a seat, because if you're keeping us standing we're not going to stop.' And then we found chairs being spread out. But they [the AEU stewards] thought 'God, you shouldn't have said that to him, it was sacrilegious'.[19]

Bevin addresses the Labour Party conference in 1945

1945 Labour victory

This change in attitudes towards their 'betters' on the part of millions of workers during the war was no doubt one of the causes of the sensational General Election result of 1945, which saw the war hero Churchill evicted from office and the first ever majority Labour government come to power, with an immense parliamentary majority. This landslide has often been attributed to the 'soldiers' vote', as people in the services determined that there would be no return to bleak 1930s Toryism, but the impetus for

Bevin speaks, Herbert Morrison listens – it was not always thus

change was at least as much due to the transformation of lives and experiences on the home front, including in the factories. It was there that the fear and social deference that had underpinned both management's 'right to manage' and the establishment's 'right to rule' began to be eroded.

Labour also came to power with a more radical and far-reaching programme than any the party had previously adopted, and this owed much to pressure from the unions, which overcame the timidity of some of the parliamentary leaders. The Trade Union Congress had called for the extension of public ownership, with public control in other industries; the establishment of a National Industrial Council; price controls; and a National Investment Board. Equally radical demands were canvassed in respect of social policy, health and welfare.[20]

This seemed at the time to represent the culmination of generations of effort by the labour movement. From the neglected and oppressed margins of society, trade unions had risen to become an acknowledged power in the land, entrenched throughout industrial life, and had now secured an electoral landslide for their own political party. It seemed to many that some form of socialism was to be established in Britain – indeed, even some amongst the upper orders faced the prospect with a weary resignation. 'We are the masters now' was the phrase somewhat inaccurately attributed to one of the new ministers, Hartley Shawcross. It is small wonder that Francis Williams entitled his official history of the TUC, published a few years later, *Magnificent Journey*. Life was, however, to prove more complicated.

Notes

1. Williams, p417.
2. Allen, p105.
3. Bullock, pp641, 650.
4. Bullock, pp652-3.
5. Allen, p230.

6. Calder, p118; Coates/Topham, p836.
7. Williams, pp418ff.
8. Allen, pp174-75.
9. Jones, p103.
10. Hutt, p151; Fuller, pp175, 181.
11. Jones, pp102, 104.
12. Jones, p107.
13. Croucher, pp79, 277.
14. Calder, p465; Croucher, p274.
15. Croucher, p266.
16. Jones, p113; Croucher, p268.
17. Croucher, p59; Allen, p225; Jones, pp87, 104.
18. Calder, p455.
19. Croucher, pp60-61.
20. Hutt, p166.

4. Cold war trade unionism 1945–1956

The change in government was mirrored by changes at the T&G, as the war in Europe ended and the war in the east moved towards its thermonuclear conclusion. In the few weeks between the formal end of the wartime coalition government and the general election which propelled Labour to power, Bevin returned to his old seat at Transport House. It is unclear whether he did anything in this brief time other than irritate Arthur Deakin.

Bevin could not have remained long at his T&G post in any case, since he would reach the retirement age of 65 in March 1946. In the event, he was summoned back to cabinet by Attlee, to take up the unexpected post of Foreign Secretary. Bevin was the first working-class man to hold this great office of state – albeit one who ended up following a foreign policy of which the establishment thoroughly approved. Deakin was thereupon elected as General Secretary of the union – a function he had been carrying out to all intents and purposes from 1940. He won with 58.5 per cent of the 347,523 votes cast by the membership, which was by then over one million strong.[1]

As a consequence of this, the T&G greeted the bright new world of the post-1945 Labour government, with all its hopes of sweeping social change, under the most reactionary leadership of its history. For the following ten years, the negative tendencies already identified in the union's structure, bureaucracy and prevailing outlook extended without hindrance, while the positive element of

Bevin's legacy and the achievements of the pre-war and wartime years were sharply curtailed.

Arthur Deakin

Arthur Deakin was, in one sense, amply prepared for his job. He had been acting general secretary, with limited interference from Bevin, for five years, and had worked as assistant general secretary for several years before that. He had studied Bevin's methods and was imbued with his outlook. His experiences were different however. Brought up in poverty in South Wales, he had been employed in the tinplate industry from an early age – a job which, in that part of the world, led to membership of the old Dockers' Union and subsequently the T&G. While South Wales was famed for the militancy of its miners, this seems not to have rubbed off on Deakin. Nor was he shaped by the atmosphere of the docks, as so many other T&G leaders had been. He had not been associated with any major strike movements, and his view of trade unionism was therefore shaped by Bevin's bureaucratic and authoritarian tendencies of the 1930s, without possessing his predecessor's hinterland of understanding of working-class struggle.

Jack Jones was clear as to the essential difference between the T&G's first two general secretaries:

> Bevin, although he was very conscious of his own importance, at least had got a considerable degree of ability and he'd done a lot in the early development of the trade union, whereas Deakin assumed the role without much background, frankly, and was rather limited in his outlook. He was never anything like Bevin in terms of ability and in terms of drive. He inherited Bevin's idea of being himself the dominant force … How the hell he ever got the general secretaryship I don't know – probably because whatever Bevin had said he agreed with.[2]

In his autobiography Jones wrote of Deakin:

He was an awkward, intolerant man ... in running the union Deakin resembled a small businessman in outlook, rather than the leader of hundreds of thousands of industrial workers ... deep down there was a gentleness which occasionally revealed itself. I formed the impression that he was a shy man who put on bluff and bluster as a front, although any liberal tendencies he may have had in his early years he brutally suppressed.[3]

Arthur Deakin in full flow

Even the most sympathetic author to have written about Deakin, Vic Allen, acknowledged that he was 'authoritarian by nature ... he had the utmost faith in his own simple, straightforward opinions and ideas'; and he noted that Deakin had devoted considerable energy to the accretion of power within the union. Still more than Bevin, Deakin regarded any form of opposition as not merely disloyalty to the organisation, but as a profound personal slight as well.[4]

Ironically, in view of Deakin's staunch and ultimately obsessive anti-Communism, one of the few in the movement to see a different side of the man was Arthur Horner, a Communist leader of the National Union of Mineworkers at that time. Horner's family had adopted the orphaned Deakin when he was a child, leading to a lifelong friendship between the two. Deakin would drive Horner home after TUC General Council meetings while continuing his anti-communist tirades (from which Horner was often explicitly exempted). 'I honestly don't believe he realised what it was all about,' Horner wrote. 'I don't think Arthur Deakin was really political at all. He tried to imitate Ernest Bevin and was just taken for a ride by much more subtle right-wing leaders, both political and industrial.'[5]

Certainly, Deakin's approach to running the union rested on more than just authoritarianism, whether instinctive or imitative. It also reflected his view of the world and the place of trade unions within it. Allen sums up the Deakin outlook well:

> He wanted no radical changes in the ownership of industry during the war nor in its methods of organisation ... He came to believe that social and economic inequities were not inherent in the type of capitalist economy in which he lived; that they could be removed by adaptations without disturbing the framework of society.

Allen's view was that Deakin did not believe at any time in the validity of class conflict in a capitalist society.[6]

The new general secretary's credo was modest and turned on preserving the living standards of T&G members without excessive exertion to actually improve them; supporting such measures of planning and social intervention as a Labour government might propose; and placing trade unionism in a context of responsibility to the wider community – a view unexceptional in and of itself but which, in Deakin's case, inexorably led to confusing the interests of the community with those of the establishment.[7]

This outlook – a limited one compared to that of Bevin before him, and Cousins, Jones and Todd later – was no doubt the product of many factors, among them the influence of Bevin in his later years of union leadership, and the fact that Deakin had never personally taken part in any major struggles or led a significant strike. But it also reflected views more widespread in the movement – that the election of a Labour government guaranteed the resolution of all pressing social problems and that, even if difficulties remained, loyalty to Labour must take precedence over any other consideration. This did not give rise to any acute problems in the first years of the Attlee government, when major industries were being nationalised and the foundations of the welfare state were being laid. But as economic difficulties mounted (and with them government pressure for wage restraint from the unions), and the Cold War began to freeze over internationally, a position of over-riding solidarity with the government was bound to lead to more right-wing views prevailing.

Of course, the T&G was very far from being the only trade union with a right-wing leadership at the time – Tewson at the TUC, Williamson at the GMWU and Lawther at the NUM were also bitter opponents of anything novel, radical or democratic. But the T&G's ties to the government were particularly strong, given Bevin's eminence within it. As Foreign Secretary, Bevin simply transferred the anti-Communism which had become a major part of his outlook in the trade union movement in the 1930s to the world scale. According to Horner, Bevin 'knew little about foreign affairs': 'the

Foreign Office, the generals and the rest played all the time on his anti-communism. They could always persuade him that, anywhere in the world where they wanted him to take a certain line, there were communist plots going on'. As a later trade union leader joked, 'to Bevin, even the Soviet Union was a breakaway from the T&G'.[8]

As Foreign Secretary he worked 'to harness the trade union movement by and large to a Churchillian foreign policy ... pro-American, anti-Soviet and actively hostile to the new popular movements that were everywhere arising against the bankrupt old order', to quote one Communist historian.[9]

And while to a generation which has only known the neo-liberalism of Tony Blair's New Labour government, or even to one which can remember no further than the storm-tossed Wilson and Callaghan years, the Attlee government may seem bathed in a glow of socialist achievement, this was not necessarily the unanimous view within the labour movement of the time. Of course, the creation of the National Health Service was a great achievement, as were other welfare reforms, and the nationalisation of several key industries could have laid the basis for more sweeping changes in the way the country was run. And, it should be noted, the government retained the overwhelming support of working-class opinion. However, as Ken Fuller has written: 'instead of socialism, the government followed a pattern which would be repeated by future Labour governments: concessions to sections of the working class, following which it buckled down to the task of managing capitalism'.[10]

Deakin's views were therefore well-attuned to those of the government as the latter moderated its social programme under budgetary pressure caused by British participation in the Korean War (1950-53); dropped further nationalisation proposals; and started to demand wage restraint from the working class to balance the national books.

In 1945 Deakin was arguing for a statutory guaranteed weekly wage in all industries, but against any state-directed incomes policy.

By the end of the decade he had reversed his position on both issues and was arguing hard (and successfully within the T&G) for wage restraint, and against a national minimum wage on the grounds that it might soon become a maximum. Vic Allen takes the view that Deakin was actually against increased wages, believing that this would lead to inflation, and preferred to see prices reduced as a result of increased productivity. The TUC's 1949 decision to support wage restraint owed much to him.

Although eventually won over to wage control, he was against any similar controls on profits, since he feared that the least efficient firms might shut down with consequential job losses. He was also firmly opposed to the idea that workers should gain any special advantage from nationalisation of the industries in which they worked – in the T&G's case this affected road haulage, taken into public ownership by the 1945 government.[11]

Deakin's T&G

These twin tendencies – authoritarianism and collaboration with employers – seeped outwards and downwards through the T&G from the General Secretary's office, above all through its large apparatus of full-time officers. According to Jones:

> the record of a lot of full-time officials was not good at that time. They tended to be somehow or other bosses' men because it was easier to agree with them than the people they were supposed to be representing ... the union was controlled by people who had been influenced rather by being bosses themselves and inclined to appease bosses and that I'm afraid went for Bevin and Arthur Deakin.[12]

In 1943 the T&G employed around 500 officers and as many staff. By 1954, the total employed had risen to 1,434, which even Deakin was beginning to think was a bit bloated – 'sapping the vitality of our people' by making them over-dependent on the full-time officers. Of course most of those officers were decent and diligent men (still very few women), but any democratic tendencies amongst them, or any view leading to confrontation with employers, even when that was the members' clear wish, met determined opposition from Deakin. Under the circumstances, many officials simply adapted to the regime.[13]

Stories abound of Deakin intervening over the heads of officials to force workers on strike back to their jobs. Management at Humber-Rootes attempted to cut back on piece-work rates established during the war thereby provoking a 'go slow', which was then followed by the announcement of 1,300 redundancies. The resulting strike was eventually successful, in spite of Deakin trying to force a return to work. Harry Nicholas, then the Engineering Group National Secretary dispatched to the Midlands to enforce Deakin's orders, was rebuked by the General Secretary on his return, not only for failing to secure an end to the strike but also for drinking with shop stewards while out in the field![14]

Frank Cousins, national official in the road transport group at the time, had the same difficulty with Deakin when London lorry drivers struck unofficially over shorter hours and more holidays in 1947, and later when trying to fight the dismissal of trade unionists at Unilever. At Unilever, he only managed to overcome the problem by daring Deakin to go down and meet the workers face to face. When London bus and tram workers struck in January 1949 and again in September 1950, Deakin was once more eager to side with the employers in the face of what was unofficial action, telling the members that he would 'not move one finger' to assist them until they returned to work.[15]

This is to some extent therefore a picture of a union which had turned into its opposite; it seemed to have become a machine for policing the working class, and enforcing their acquiescence in policies and management conduct that was detrimental to their interests and in opposition to their own wishes. But, as ever, the

Transport and General Workers' Record

❈ ❈ ❈ ❈

Official Organ of the Transport and General Workers' Union

(Known in Ireland as the "Amalgamated Transport and General Workers' Union")

Editorial Office : Transport House, Smith Square, Westminster, S.W.1

| VOL. XXX—No. 343 | JUNE, 1950 | Price Twopence |

"On the Job"

MAKING
NYLONS

Photo by
Tulse Vale Studios

Putting women on the cover

reality is more nuanced. In some cases, including two of those cited above, Deakin had to back down from his initial position when confronted by determined members allied to a sympathetic officer. Officers with principle could, if they were sure of their ground, stand up to Deakin and survive. This was not a union without any life in it. And it should also be acknowledged that, like Bevin before him, Deakin had to secure the support of committees and conferences of lay members for his views and attitudes, including his view that it was the job of those same members to faithfully follow the lead he gave. Nor was Deakin himself invariably reactionary. In 1950 he reaffirmed the T&G's commitment to equal pay and equal opportunities for women, and the following year he gave successful backing to the membership in a dispute in the road haulage industry – although he insisted that this forthright support, expressed in a meeting with government ministers, was kept quiet, since 'even when he sympathised with a strike Deakin could scarcely bear to admit it publicly', in Goodman's words.[16]

The post-war T&G continued to organise extensively. It needed to – the union was afflicted by a very high membership turnover, having to recruit over 480,000 new members in 1947 to show a net gain of just 44,000. Most of the growth continued to come in the same industries that had provided the basis for the membership increases in the 1930s and during the war, and things were made easier by the fact that, unlike the situation after the First World War, full employment was maintained and industry continued to work at something like full tilt.[17]

The T&G played a major part in the ultimately successful struggle – conducted before during and after the war – to unionise the Ford motor company, and in particular its giant plant at Dagenham on the Thames estuary. A decisive role was played by Irish workers, who struck in support of a victimised shop steward in the foundry.

The T&G engaged in very few mergers with other unions during Deakin's time in office, and those that were accomplished were relatively minor and local. This may itself have reflected Deakin's awkwardness of personality, since establishing amicable relations at the top is often critical in securing union amalgamations. At any event, he was clear that there was to be no progress on the perennial issue of uniting with the other great general union: 'I can say very clearly that amalgamation with the NUGMW will never happen. Their constitution is totally different', he predicted in 1944 and to date he has been proved right.[18]

Docks turmoil

After the war some of the gains secured for workers under wartime conditions were made permanent, reflecting the strength provided to workers by full employment and the relatively benign political environment created by the new government. Among these gains were joint committees of employers and unions in the shipbuilding and engineering industries to regulate pay and conditions, established in 1947.

One of the most important advances for the T&G was the Dock Workers (Regulation of Employment) Act, which established the National Dock Labour Scheme. This scheme introduced some measure of decasualisation in the industry at long last and guaranteed dockers payment for being available for work. Dockers remained at the heart of the T&G and, during the period of Deakin's leadership, they were once more the union's most militant section. The docks group had around 85,000 members at the time, 65,000 of them in ports covered by the new Dock Labour Scheme. They were serviced by 90 full-time officers, with 34 others dealing with docks as part of their allocation. There were 21 docks officers in Liverpool alone and 15 in the Port of London, looking after 15,000 and 17,000 members respectively. However, there were still thousands of dockers in other unions as well, from the GMWU in the north-east to the lightermen and stevedores in London, the coal-trimmers in Cardiff and the breakaway Scottish TGWU in the

Glasgow docks. This provided continuing opportunities for inter-union friction.[19]

Strong local traditions remained across the industry, rooted in the widely varying conditions from one port and one employer to another – there were differences in docking facilities, the nature of the cargoes handled and the organisation of work. So the National Dock Labour Scheme was no panacea for industrial relations difficulties in the industry. Indeed, suspicion that the scheme might be an excuse for the imposition of an onerous level of labour discipline caused difficulties in some ports – London and Tilbury dockers had struck for a week in March 1945 over this issue.

Major labour disputes in the docks became a regular feature of post-war industrial life, straining relations between the workers and the government and within the T&G, which under Deakin frowned on almost any form of industrial action, and unofficial action most of all. Strong unofficial leadership among the dockers emerged in many ports, London and Liverpool most notably – in spite of (or perhaps because of) the large number of full-time officials allocated to them. The establishment increasingly took fright at this situation, at a time when any disruption to trade was presented as a national emergency. One report of an official inquiry complained: 'It appears to be incredibly easy to bring dock workers out on strike. We were given repeated instances of men stopping work almost automatically, with little or no idea why they were stopping.' This contemptuous attitude towards the dockers and their grievances was buttressed by the use of the wartime Emergency Works Orders which, having been deployed very sparingly during the war itself, were now regularly invoked by the Attlee government against peacetime industrial action in the docks.[20]

A national docks strike in September 1945 over wages lasted for six weeks. A further dispute in London in June 1948, which brought together many of the problems besetting industrial relations in the ports, is described by Hutt:

A local dispute, pursued through the normal channels, over the rate to be paid for handling a cargo of zinc oxide, was followed by the suspension of certain of the men concerned; the strike flared up against what was claimed to be the arbitrary use by the National Dock Labour Board of its disciplinary powers. Before the strike ended it had spread to Merseyside, some 30,000 dockers were affected, the government had sent troops to the docks and had proclaimed a State of Emergency.[21]

The stoppages in May and June 1949 in support of the Canadian Seamen's Union strike over wage cuts were even more dramatic. Several ports were brought to a halt under the leadership of unofficial committees acting against the advice of their officers. This dispute was, in Hutt's words, 'one of the most historic struggles ever waged by the dockers or any other section of British workers. The issue was not one of wages or conditions but of international working-class solidarity'.

It began when Avonmouth dockers refused to unload one vessel which had a scab crew, whereupon the port employers declared a lock out. The smuggling of a Canadian cargo to Liverpool spread the strike to Merseyside, where 11,000 dockers went out; and then to London where more than 15,000 stopped work. In the end the Canadian seamen secured terms and asked for the solidarity action to be stood down, but not before troops were once more deployed along the dockside amidst a mounting red-baiting hysteria. In the intensifying cold war climate, these demonstrations of solidarity were seen as treason by the government, the press and sections of the T&G leadership alike. Deakin claimed that in London the unofficial strike committee numbered 36 Communists or 'fellow travellers' out of its membership of 48. Of course the 'fellow travelling' label could be applied to almost anyone under such circumstances, and was a device to avoid confronting the actual issues involved in any dispute. It was against this background that one of the most infamous attacks on union democracy in the T&G was initiated.[22]

Anti-Communism

The TUC had started its effort to drive Communists out of the trade union movement back in the 1930s, with a 'black circular' suggesting that affiliates should exclude Communist Party members from all office. The T&G under Bevin took exception to this suggestion and ignored it, less for want of anti-Communist enthusiasm on Bevin's part than from resentment at any idea of the TUC interfering in his union, allied perhaps to an appreciation of the Communists' organising efforts in the T&G at the time. After the war the T&G was the exception in the other direction, since most of the principal unions refused to outlaw Communists and repudiated witch-hunts, despite encouragement from Congress House. Deakin, however, was a man on a mission.[23]

The Communist Party of Great Britain had nothing like the mass following of Communist parties in much of continental Europe at the time. Membership at the end of the war was around 50,000 and its parliamentary representation was just two. Communist Party affiliation to the Labour Party had been rejected. The proposal to support affiliation was defeated at the 1945 T&G conference by 352 to 208 after a strong personal intervention by Bevin himself.[24] However, the party had considerable strength in the trade union movement, not least among sections covered by the T&G in the docks, London Buses and the motor and engineering industries. Party members were active in pushing for a militant policy of working-class advance and were prepared to organise and initiate action through unofficial structures when the established union channels were not responsive. These attitudes had long caused friction with Bevin and Deakin, but it took the atmosphere of the Cold War to bring the tension to fever pitch.

Graham Stevenson, himself a T&G national official in a later epoch, expresses the prevailing atmosphere: 'the assumption [was] that war with the Soviet Union was inevitable, that the CPGB was a direct instrument of Soviet policy and ... because of this it constituted a danger to national security, which excused anything.'[25]

These assumptions established the firmest of holds on the thinking of Arthur Deakin, who disliked strikes under any circumstances, and unofficial committees even more. That Communists should be involved in both developed in his imagination to such an extent that an issue concerning industrial and trade union procedures transformed itself into something more akin to high treason. 'The Communist Party stands indicted as the declared enemy of the British working class,' he declared in 1948; and later he stated that the Communists' 'avowed intention was to do all possible to retard the nation's recovery'.[26]

In addition to his opposition to any group that he saw as using the T&G for its own political purposes, and to any members who employed 'unconstitutional' methods and might have an external call on their loyalty, there was undoubtedly a personal edge to Deakin's venom. After the war there were nine Communists on the T&G General Executive Council and they were not backward in criticising the General Secretary's conduct of affairs. Nothing could have been more intolerable to him.

The General Secretary denounced the Communist Party for even having a view on industrial matters: 'how long has it been the prerogative or duty of any political party to devise charters relating to the wages and conditions of workpeople who are well organised within their own trade unions?' he asked. Of course, Communist action derived much of its strength from the widespread and not unjustified belief within the T&G that workpeople were *not* being well served by their union organisation.[27]

Increasingly, Deakin came to see the hand of Communists behind any industrial disruption at all, and became blind to the real grievances of working people. As much as any business leader, he equated strikes with communism. He viewed independent left-wing officials like Frank Cousins as little better than Communists, truly coming to see a 'red' under every 'bed'. Of course, it was true that

Communists were involved in many disputes, and generally were thorough, disciplined and effective leaders of strikes, official or unofficial; and through these successes they attracted the support of wide sections of the working class, as industrial if not often political leaders. But this could only occur on the basis of real grievances requiring redress among the mass membership.

Deakin placed himself at the head of the onslaught against Communists in the trade union movement both nationally and internationally. According to Hutt, 'on every conceivable occasion he attacked them for their activities and motives'. Deakin took the leading part in organising a split in the World Federation of Trade Unions, organising an Anglo-American walk-out from the global body.[28]

In the T&G, the anti-communist campaign culminated in a plan to drive Party members out of any position within the union. The 1949 Biennial Delegate Conference debated a rule banning Communists being either full-time officers or lay officials from the start of 1950. This was accepted by 426 votes against 208, although most of the debate ran against the proposed witch-hunt. The decision had the effect of denying very large sections of the union's membership the right to choose their own preferred officials. Fascists were also notionally covered by the ban, but this was a mere smokescreen and no fascist was ever disciplined under its provisions, since the far right had not then – nor ever before or since – secured as much as a toehold in the T&G.[29]

Nine full-time officers who refused to renounce their membership of the Communist Party were thereupon dismissed fairly brutally, although the BDC had probably not intended that serving officers should be sacked. Their jobs were advertised before their appeals against dismissal had even been heard. Numerous lay activists, from GEC members downwards, were also excluded from all positions and systematically hounded throughout the union, with some being called upon to 'prove' that they were not members of the Communist Party. One hundred and four branches sent in protests against the witch-hunt, as did two national committees (passenger and chemical) and the Scottish regional committee. A lobby of Transport House against the ban ended with Communist cab driver Sid Easton grabbing Deakin by the throat after the latter had called the protestors 'scum'.[30]

The ban had a particularly negative effect in the passenger group, whose national secretary, Sam Henderson, was removed from office – as was much of the lay leadership in the London Bus section. In the words of Larry Smith, later an assistant general secretary of the union, Henderson was 'the most popular officer'. 'The lads identified with him and felt that he was the best leader that they had had ... the members were enraged about the ban'. In this way, Deakinism deeply damaged the work of the union. It is small surprise that one London bus branch voted 56 to nil against the proposition that 'the Transport and General Workers' Union is a democratic organisation', despite the regional passenger group secretary's attendance to speak in favour of the motion. Henderson's successor as national secretary – and other Deakin appointees – presided over a rapid decline in London taxi cab membership and organisation, a decline from which the T&G never fully recovered.[31]

As Deakin's biographer mildly puts it:

> All told, the Union went into a phase of orthodoxy in the opinions expressed in it and in the decisions it recorded ... the public picture emerged of Deakin as a man with an anti-Communist phobia which prevented his seeing real grievances when they existed. And for this he was treated less seriously.[32]

The end of the Deakin era

As the 1950s wore on, the ground started to shift under Deakinism. The political and industrial landscape was changing. After Labour lost office in 1951, Deakin hastened to assure the new Tory administration that 'we shall not be guilty of fractious opposition to the government merely for the sake of playing politics', and he devoted his political energies instead to trying to hound Aneurin Bevan and his supporters out of the Labour Party. But with Labour in opposition, and the Cold War abating somewhat with the end of hostilities in Korea, the political aspects of Deakin's approach seemed increasingly anachronistic.[33]

Industrially, passivity was on the way out. Full employment gave workers the confidence to fight back against employers still clinging to the master-servant attitudes of the pre-war period. In 1953 Jack Jones led a successful struggle to oppose 1000 redundancies at Morris Engines plant, challenging management's right to sack whoever it wanted, much to their stupefaction. With management's divine right to manage being contested in the factories, the same workers were not likely to acquiesce in the officials' divine right to lead within their own union, particularly when the results of such leadership were so meagre.[34]

Deakin himself was incapable of adapting. Stevenson argues that by the time of his death in 1955, his regime 'had brought the union close to disintegration', largely through his 'absurd anti-communism'. This may seem a slightly extravagant judgement, bearing in mind that the T&G remained in the mid-1950s a formidable industrial apparatus – but behind the imposing bureaucratic structure a rot had definitely set in. As one symptom of this, no fewer than 10,000 dockers quit the union in 1954, mainly in Hull, Liverpool and Manchester, in a row provoked and prolonged by Deakin's intransigent resistance to any action to address their festering grievances. The recalcitrant dockers joined the rival Stevedores Union, leading to the latter's suspension from the TUC. This action may have upheld the integrity of trade union procedures, but it did not persuade the northern dockers to rejoin the T&G. It is possible that a prolongation of Deakin's methods might have led to further defections and a serious crisis in the union, beyond the reach of resolution by his preferred methods of authoritarian bullying.[35]

Arthur Deakin (centre) with the candidates to succeed him in 1955, including Jock Tiffin (second left), Harry Nicholas (third left) and Frank Cousins (far right)

In the event, Deakin died in 1955, just as the election for his successor was taking place. Deakin's legacy to trade unionism is almost entirely a negative one, his style of leadership a litany of what is to be avoided rather than emulated. Nevertheless, many of those who have studied the man insist that there was a far warmer and more generous individual lurking behind the blustering and intolerant exterior than is generally acknowledged. Frank Cousins, on taking office later, discovered many examples of kind and charitable acts towards individuals by Deakin, acts he was most concerned to keep private. As Geoffrey Goodman observes, Deakin's flaws were 'almost always on public display and he never apologised for them. His warmer, more human qualities were concealed.'[36]

Arthur 'Jock' Tiffin, who had been serving as assistant general secretary since succeeding Harold Clay in that post in 1948, was elected to the top job, becoming the T&G's third general secretary.

He defeated five other officials in the election, including Frank
Cousins and Harry Nicholas. Tiffin, who had previously worked as
a bus driver and as an official in the union's London/South-Eastern
region, would probably have moved away from Deakin's precepts
fairly rapidly, but he did not live long enough to establish the point,
dying of cancer just six months into his term of office. Alas, he is
remembered largely for having the briefest term as T&G general
secretary of any holder of the job.

Jack Jones wrote of Tiffin:

> I found him to be very critical of Deakin's dictatorial character.
> Tiffin wanted changes in the union, especially freer exchanges of
> opinion and more attention to union education. Politically a
> 'middle of the road' man and a traditionalist whose attitude had
> … been shaped by the fact that he gained an army commission in
> the First World War, Tiffin nevertheless sensed that the union was
> too bureaucratic, with a wide gap between the leaders and the
> membership.[37]

Jock Tiffin was not able to implement any of the changes he may
have wished for. But the scene was now set for the most profound
transformation in the T&G since its formation.

Notes

1. Allen, p230.
2. Geoffrey Goodman interview.
3. Jones, pp132-33.
4. Allen, p257.
5. Horner, p183.
6. Allen, p113.
7. Allen, p116.
8. Horner, p183.
9. Hutt, p173.
10. Fuller, p189.
11. Allen, pp121-131.
12. Geoffrey Goodman interview.

13. Allen, p248.
14. Jones, p122.
15. Goodman, pp64-65, 88; Allen, pp168-69.
16. Allen, p171; Goodman, p91.
17. Allen, p241; Croucher, p316.
18. Allen, p156.
19. Allen, pp172, 176-77.
20. Allen, p196.
21. Hutt, p182.
22. Allen, p277.
23. Hutt, p178.
24. Allen, p271.
25. Stevenson, p30.
26. Allen, p270; Stevenson, p31.
27. Allen, p275.
28. Allen, p280.
29. Allen, p284.
30. Easton/Stevenson, pp18/19.
31. Fuller, pp195-7.
32. Allen, p288.
33. Allen, p150.
34. Jones, p129.
35. Stevenson, p41.
36. Goodman, p101.
37. Jones, p142.

5. A progressive union 1956-1969

The watershed in the T&G's history represented by the election of Frank Cousins as General Secretary in 1956 was in one sense inevitable and in another entirely fortuitous.

The element of chance had arisen from the appointment of Jock Tiffin as the union's assistant general secretary several years earlier. Harry Nicholas, a national secretary favoured by Deakin, had been front-runner for the position, but had been found ineligible to stand, owing to a small gap in his union contributions record. This minor blemish had been caused by a difficult period of hospitalisation for Nicholas's wife, but rules were rules and his candidacy could not be considered. This led to the promotion of Tiffin in his place, and, once ensconced as number two, Tiffin progressed naturally to number one after Deakin's departure. Had Deakin been replaced by the hale and hearty Nicholas, Cousins would almost certainly never have had his crack at the top job.

So much for individual destiny. But the necessity for a new departure for the T&G was etched into the changing industrial and political environment, which was increasingly making the bilious authoritarianism of Deakin (and his ilk in other trade unions) an anachronism. Full employment was bolstering working-class confidence, and the experiences of the war, further fortified by some of the social gains introduced by the 1945 Labour government, were sweeping away the traditions of deference in factory, society and the unions alike. In the context of the T&G, the development of the shop stewards movement in the rapidly growing motor and engineering industries enhanced democratic tendencies, and these, allied to the traditionally militant sections such as the docks and passenger transport, undermined the basis for any continuation of the methods of Bevin and Deakin. As Geoffrey Goodman observes

in the mid-fifties a new dimension of tension began to develop on the shop-floor; unofficial strikes increased sharply and many of them were as much a protest against what was increasingly seen as a remoteness of trade union officialdom as they were demonstrations against the traditional foes, the employer. A new degree of shop-floor assertiveness was growing, and as it developed it infected the younger generation of workers with a fresh sense of awareness and confidence.[1]

Frank Cousins

Cousins caught this tide. To cite his outstanding biographer Goodman once more: 'If it hadn't been Cousins, then it is almost certain that these changes would have thrown up someone else who would have understood the impulses of the moment, and would have been able to respond to them.'[2] Jack Jones shares this view: 'It was a sign of the times. Rank-and-file members wanted changes.' But Jones adds an important caveat: 'The union's policies did not switch from left to right overnight with his election. Many of the officers and branches remained faithful to the traditional right-wing policies of the union.'[3]

Indeed, the attempt led by Frank Cousins to shape a new, forward-looking and more combative T&G met with serious opposition, not merely from employers and government, from whom it might have been expected, but also from the establishment in the trade union movement, and from many officials in the T&G itself (all of whom had of course been appointed under Bevin or

Deakin). According to Goodman: 'They tended to have a strong vested interest in the *status quo*, and those who were ready to welcome change were reluctant to move either as swiftly or as boldly as Cousins wished'. Goodman saw this as 'a huge and discouraging handicap' for the newly-elected General Secretary.

Life had prepared Cousins well for the challenge. He left school at fourteen to work in a Yorkshire coal mine but had quit the pit for a job in road haulage from 1923. Then as now, lorry driving was a highly demanding job, in an industry full of rapacious employers. By its nature it is a difficult industry in which to build the strong collective spirit that emerges more spontaneously among dockers, car workers or bus drivers, who work together in large numbers at a common location. The T&G's road transport (commercial) group was nevertheless a central one throughout the union's history.

Cousins joined the union in 1933 and was appointed a full-time official in 1938, as South Yorkshire district organiser for the road transport trade group. He was named national secretary of the road transport (commercial) group ten years later, an appointment which led, as noted in the previous chapter, to a number of clashes with Arthur Deakin, with whom he had a fraught, if respectful, relationship. The general secretary suspected Cousins, accurately, of holding radical political views, and he certainly deplored his tendency to support industrial militancy on the part of the members. Cousins's success in securing the assistant general secretary position upon Jock Tiffin's election to replace Deakin was a tribute to his immense personal qualities, which overcame the reluctance of more conservative elements in the T&G. When Tiffin died, Cousins was certainly well placed to succeed him, since the number two could expect to secure the support of most leading officials to take over when the top vacancy arose. However, his election victory – he polled over 503,560 votes to his opponent Tom Healey's 77,916, on a record turn-out – was remarkable by any standards. It was a clear indication that the rank-and-file were ready for a new approach.

The new line

The first signs of that approach emerged before Cousins had even taken office. In December 1955, when he was merely acting general secretary, he told the GEC: 'While prices rise, wages must rise with them ... we are not prepared that our members should stand still while the government continually hands out largesse to those who are more favourably placed.' Today this sounds a modest enough view for a trade unionist to advance, but at the time it marked a most radical departure in the conduct of union business. Since the Attlee government had 'sold' incomes policy to the unions six years earlier, wage restraint had become a dogma for the leadership of most unions. As we have seen, Deakin was almost *opposed* to higher wages, believing that price reductions were more desirable and that a 'disciplined' approach to wages, even at the expense of members' living standards, was an earnest of trade unions' responsibility and fitness to be admitted into the leading counsels of the nation.

Such an approach was debilitating enough with Labour in power, but it became doubly disastrous with the Tories back in office after 1951. Management in industry was still fighting for its sacred right to manage without reference to the workforce. For example, in 1956 massive lay-offs without notice were made in the midlands car industry, where the T&G (and the AEU) had been struggling to extend union organisation. This contemptuous approach to the workers (which even embarrassed government ministers) led to a strike at the British Motor Corporation's huge Longbridge plant. The dispute was supported by the union's members in the docks, the road haulage industry and passenger transport, and also saw the use of the tactic of mass picketing, possibly for the first time. The strike – a harbinger of growing conflict in car factories – secured three weeks' notice and full consultation before further dismissals, and also helped set the context for the industrial policies Cousins was to follow. In 1957 there were major strikes among engineering workers, provincial bus workers, dockers and market porters, and overall days lost to industrial action hit a post-war high.[5]

The new 'members-first' approach faced its most significant challenge in 1958, when London bus workers took their first strike action since the 'Coronation' dispute twenty-one years previously. The issue was pay restraint, aggressively introduced by Harold Macmillan's Tory government and just as firmly rejected by the T&G, on the grounds that it placed the entire burden for solving the country's economic problems on the workers. Fifty-three thousand members walked out after their modest pay claim was rejected. Cousins tried to rally broader support for the members, explaining that the busworkers were fighting not for themselves alone but for all underpaid and underprivileged workers whose wages were falling behind the cost of living, as a result of government interference in industrial negotiations. The strike lasted seven weeks. However it failed to break the pay restraint policy and was largely defeated.

This was to a significant extent due to the machinations of a right-wing TUC leadership, who were not at all unhappy to see Cousins, the new radical, undermined. According to Tory minister Iain Macleod, who was secretly visited by TUC leaders to secure that end while the strike was on: 'They wanted Cousins taken down a peg. They didn't like him. They wanted to ensure that the government didn't cave in'. In fact, the integrity and commitment Cousins showed throughout the strike left his stature enhanced, rather than diminished, and the dispute helped to irrevocably change 'the relationship between leadership and led in the TGWU', in Goodman's words.[6]

T&G organisation expanded in this new atmosphere of mounting militancy and greater unity between members and leaders. An ex-commando sergeant named Alan Law became legendary in the Midlands for his efforts in organising lorry drivers. According to Jones, then the union's Midlands regional secretary, Law was 'a tearaway, unpredictable type'. 'He swept down the haulage companies like a tornado. He led a movement that brought organisation among the lorry drivers and car delivery workers to a high level'. Membership

1956: the picket line at Cowley …

… and at Longbridge

Voting for action at Standard Motors, Coventry

grew sharply, reaching more than 1.3 million in 1960, a consequence of both buoyant employment and the union's more assertive approach to addressing members' problems.[7]

Growth through mergers was also resumed, with the Scottish Textile Workers joining in 1961 and, two years later, the trade unions in Gibraltar all agreeing to amalgamate with the T&G, establishing the union as the major industrial force in this imperial outpost. And, in a further sign of the union's extending influence, a strike by Heathrow Airport loaders in 1961 won a substantial wage increase. This was far from the last major struggle the union had to fight at the airports. Civil aviation was to grow in importance in the T&G as the industry rapidly expanded. John Cousins recalls: 'When I started at Heathrow Airport we had five thousand members, and when I'd left we had got over fifteen thousand'. Gains were also won for traditional sectors of the union, including a 40-hour week for the dockers, achieved in 1963.[8]

Conflict continued in the docks throughout the 1960s, however. A report by Lord Devlin which urged decasualisation of dock work – a historic T&G objective of course – provoked years of strife, because it handed greater disciplinary powers to employers at the expense of the National Dock Labour Board, and, above all, because it was bound up with the drive to containerisation, which spelt doom for thousands of jobs in the ports. London, Liverpool and Hull were particularly militant, but Cousins avoided the splits which might well have resulted from this situation (and almost certainly would have done under Deakin) by dealing with the dockers' 'unofficial leadership', headed by Communists like the famous Jack Dash – for some time the media's 'most hated man in Britain' – and endeavouring to secure consensus. Soon, however, port employment was to go into rapid free-fall, changing forever the nature of dockside communities – the soil from which the T&G had sprung.

The new line in politics

While Cousins's impact on the bread-and-butter issues of trade unionism was profound, he is perhaps better remembered for his political role, and in particular his opposition to nuclear weapons and support for socialist principles, at a time when both were subject to bitter debate within the Labour Party. These positions marked the inauguration of the T&G's left-wing political tradition, a tradition which has been broadly maintained ever since, and has seen the union established as a major element in progressive politics and public campaigning.

Both these issues arose in the context of a movement trying to grapple with significant changes in the environment around it, both domestically and on a world scale. To take the nuclear arms issue first, the abatement of the worst of the cold war confrontation and the lessening of international tension had raised anew the issue of Britain's possession of 'the bomb'.

Frank Cousins marches for nuclear disarmament

The Campaign for Nuclear Disarmament was founded in 1958 to encourage Britain to give a 'moral lead' to the world by renouncing the manufacture, deployment or use of nuclear weapons. Clearly, it was much more likely that the Labour Party could be won to this position than the Tories, and it was this that put the views of the T&G under the spotlight. Undoubtedly, the lead given by Frank Cousins was decisive. His son John, later himself a T&G national official, had backed CND from the beginning, and no doubt this influenced his father's views.

In 1959, Cousins swung the union to unilateral nuclear disarmament, describing nuclear weapons as 'not defence weapons' – nuclear weapons were 'weapons of mass suicide'. He had earlier outlined his views on the issue in the starkest terms: 'This country, if no other will do it, ought to take the moral lead ... I would remind you that it is not a set of trade union negotiations in which we are engaged ... We must say that this nation of all nations ... does not approve of the maintenance and manufacture, either by ourselves or anyone else of this idiot's weapon. There is no compromise with evil'.[9]

It is often forgotten that the GMWU conference also adopted this policy, so horrifying its right-wing leader Sir Thomas Williamson that he took the unheard-of step of summoning a recall conference to reverse the decision. But it was the T&G that took the lead and in 1960 its views became TUC policy, Cousins moving the decisive resolution, with a speech quoting the Pope, Churchill and Lord Hailsham.[10]

This set the union on a course of confrontation with the Labour Party leadership. Hugh Gaitskell was bitterly opposed to a policy that he not only rejected on principle but also regarded as a vote-loser. More surprisingly, the icon of the left Nye Bevan was also won over to this view. The split led to the most famous quotes attributed to either man – Gaitskell's pledge to 'fight, fight and fight again' on the issue, and Bevan's demand that a Labour Foreign Secretary (which he hoped to be) should not be sent 'naked into the conference chamber'. The T&G, however, carried the day at the conference, making Labour nominally committed to nuclear disarmament for a year, a position which has since recurred when the Party has been in opposition but has never been implemented (or even seriously considered) when in government.

The issue of removing Labour's Clause Four constitutional commitment to public ownership of the economy also provoked a sharp, if briefer and less personalised, debate within the labour movement. Gaitskell proposed abandoning this formal commitment in 1959, in a move that echoed similar steps being taken by the German Social Democratic Party, which around the same time had agreed to drop its notional adherence to Marxism. Gaitskell's stance also reflected the belief on Labour's right-wing that the party should move away from its traditional values and 'cloth cap image' in order to win office in a more middle-class society.

Most trade unions had doubts about this proposal, having themselves constitutional commitments to public ownership of one sort or another in their rule books. Moreover – and this is a significant point of difference between 1959 and 1995, when the debate on Clause Four was next engaged – public ownership was far from being seen as anachronistic. At the time the economic achievements of the Soviet Union were still widely admired, including by those who held no brief for its political system. And the nationalised industries in Britain itself were regarded as a progressive achievement throughout the movement, and accepted as an unavoidable feature of modern society by many outside it.

The T&G, and Cousins personally, played the leading part in demanding that the Labour Party not renounce its commitment to public ownership, while also debating what its priorities should be when it returned to government. Gaitskell soon came to realise that he had misjudged the party's mood, and his proposal was quietly allowed to drop, not to resurface again for thirty-five years.

These debates made Frank Cousins appear as a leading political figure, much more so than most contemporary trade union leaders, and a controversial one at that. But neither he nor the union were always at odds with Labour's leadership. Cousins and Gaitskell united in opposition to the proposal that Britain should join what was then known as the Common Market, a shared stand that led to a measure of a reconciliation between the two men before the Labour leader died in 1963. But it is fair to say that Cousins's assertive and occasionally abrasive presentation of the union's political views caused some unease within the union itself, and his opinions on nuclear disarmament, in particular, were not shared by all the membership. Nevertheless, like Bevin before him, he always took care to win the union's own democratic structures to his point of view through argument and debate before launching into controversy at the TUC or the Labour Party, and the T&G itself was doing no more than exercising its rights as a Labour Party affiliate. However, the sharp public controversy about the role of trade unions within the party was reignited from this period onwards. The establishment had been unconcerned about Labour's historic connection with the trade union movement while leaders like Deakin and Williamson ensured that the unions acted as guarantors of right-wing supremacy in the party, but it suddenly discovered the 'unacceptable' nature of union affiliation once they began to act as a progressive force. A union circular issued in 1960 made the point:

> It is also suggested in some quarters that the industrial interests of the membership are being subordinated to political activities. What hypocrisy! If the union had pursued a policy of support for nuclear weapons these critics would have praised our 'good sense' and 'statesmanship'. Their praise is worth as much as their criticisms. It is not the fact that we are concerned with politics that so annoys our opponents in the press world; it is because we pursue successfully policies of which they do not approve ... the General Executive Council has always taken the view that the concern for the well-being of the members cannot be restricted to purely industrial matters. Peace concerns us all and we have a duty to make our views clear.[11]

There is no doubt that this progressive alignment is the most enduring element of the Cousins legacy, in that the T&G has maintained its commitment to peace and socialism ever since, and has indeed often formed the backbone of the left in British politics, and within the Labour Party in particular. In the shorter term, the

Cousins meets Nye Bevan

Cousins campaigning for election in Nuneaton, 1965

reputation Cousins acquired as a 'politician' inevitably led to speculation, from the earliest days of his general secretaryship of the T&G, that his real destiny lay in the House of Commons and the Labour front bench. For many years, he pooh-poohed the suggestion, but that nevertheless is what eventually came to pass.

In and out of government

The proposal that Frank Cousins should become the second T&G general secretary to move into the Cabinet, should Labour be elected to government, was initially made by Hugh Gaitskell, shortly before his death in January 1963. This may seem surprising, given the deep divisions between the two over nuclear weapons and nationalisation, but the possibility was inspired by their agreement over the Common Market issue and, no doubt, by the need for the Labour Party to find a way to reunite before facing the electorate. At that stage, Cousins did not rule the idea out, and it resurfaced when Labour had a new leader in Harold Wilson, who had much better personal relations with Cousins, and who became prime minister at the end of 1964.

Cousins was offered, and accepted, the job of Minister of Technology, and a parliamentary seat was found for him at Nuneaton in a by-election early in 1965. There were indications at the time that this might not be a successful move. Certainly, there were points in its favour – the political standing of Cousins within the party and his great interest in scientific and technological issues, which chimed with Wilson's famous 'white hot technological revolution'. However, Cousins's awkward and argumentative personality did not augur well for his adaptation to the compromises and 'gentlemen's club' atmosphere of parliamentary life, very different from what he had experienced as the unchallenged leader of a huge industrial organisation. More seriously, the division over incomes policy, which ultimately precipitated his resignation from government, was already latent. The T&G led opposition within the TUC to proposals for statutory wage controls, while the Labour government, like its Tory predecessor, was obsessed with the question of pay restraint almost from the outset. Bevin's old sparring partner, Bill Jones of the London Buses, was opposed to Cousins's move to the ministry. His view was that the T&G general secretary could do more to shape the government's direction from his existing office than from parliament.[12]

Jones was in a minority on the T&G executive, however, and Cousins was given leave to join the government. But he did not resign from his union position. Like Bevin before him, he remained T&G General Secretary throughout his time in the Cabinet. Harry Nicholas moved up to become acting general secretary, *de facto* leader of the union, with Jack Jones acting as number two.

As General Secretary, therefore, Cousins had an obligation – and not one he would have wished to shirk for an instant – of continuing to represent the T&G's strong views, in particular on economic management and incomes policy. Yet he would also be bound by the inevitable discipline of collective cabinet responsibility to support agreed government decisions – and this was a government which, under Wilson's prevaricating leadership, leaned ever more decisively towards the right-wing of the party. This was a recipe for conflict and ultimate resignation almost from the start. But, as Goodman notes, 'it would be quite false … to suppose that Frank Cousins went into the Labour government without illusions … Perhaps, indeed he had too many illusions'.

The union's own views on wages were clear. Cousins wrote in the *T&G Record* in 1963: 'We are interested in securing higher real wages for our members. But while the economic conditions exist which force us to defend the living standards of our members by achieving money wage increases we shall have to do so.'[13]

And elsewhere:

When we have achieved a measure of planning and a Socialist government and, if I have to say to my members, 'we must now exercise restraint' I will say it and when I say it I will mean it …

When I talk to the government ... they are much more influenced
when I am saying the things my members want me to say. We will
not have wage restraint, whoever brings it and wraps it up for us.[14]

As this position implies, the T&G would only countenance any
planning of wages in the context of socialist planning of the
economy as a whole. That became the orthodox position of the
trade union left over the next twenty years. The difficulty was that
successive Labour governments had neither the desire nor the
capacity to bring in sweeping changes to the economic and social
system of the country. Social reforms and a bit more
nationalisation, perhaps; but the full control of the commanding
heights of the economy, breaking the economic power of capitalism
– the only circumstances under which wage restraint would not
become a synonym for wage cuts and higher profits for business –
not likely. When George Brown, then Secretary of State for
Economic Affairs in the Labour government, told the 1965 party
conference that the government had embarked on a 'financial and
economic and social revolution', to which unions should contribute
through pay restraint, he was trying to square this circle. However,
he was not telling the truth about government achievements, or
indeed its intentions.

Yet neither had the left in the Labour Party a comprehensive and
coherent programme for economic change worked out. It could
fairly be argued that Labour's 1964 parliamentary majority of four
was too small for such radicalism in any case (two right-wing
Labour MPs were sufficient to obstruct the nationalisation of the
steel industry for a time). A far bigger majority was secured in 1966,
but by then the government was already losing its sense of purpose
and sliding into (capitalist) crisis management.

Cousins's ministerial record lies outside the scope of this book.
But the growing conflict over economic and industrial policy
between on the one hand the T&G and much of the rest of the trade
union movement, and on the other the government, shaped much

of the politics of the 1960s – including, of course, the exit of Cousins from government in 1966.

By the end of 1965 the Tory press was taunting Cousins with the contradiction between the T&G's position and the government's, asserting that it was 'time to choose'. Increasingly, they were right. Cousins believed that he had secured an agreement with Wilson that a statutory pay policy would be dropped, and he campaigned in the 1966 General Election as a government minister on that basis.

General Secretary with a car industry lobby

When it emerged after the election that he had either misunderstood the Prime Minister or been duped by him (neither were uncommon occurrences in the Wilson years), his position rapidly became untenable, and it was exacerbated by his widely shared opposition to the then-escalating war in Vietnam.[15] Speaking to a T&G audience in the Midlands a fortnight before his resignation, Cousins made his priorities clear: 'I have no different views to those I had before I went into the government and if steps are taken that are in too great a conflict with union policy there need be no doubt about where I shall stand and what I shall do.'[16]

And indeed Cousins quit the government in July 1966, writing a scorching resignation letter to Wilson, in which he poured out much of his frustration at his eighteen months in government. Opposition to pay policy was not the whole story, however. Cousins was additionally concerned that if his 'leave of absence' continued much longer, pressure would become irresistible for Harry Nicholas to become General Secretary in name as well as fact. This, he feared, could lead to the T&G moving back some way towards the right,

Cousins denouncing Labour's incomes policy at the conference rostrum

if not to full-blown Deakinism, and would block the prospects for Jack Jones (already Cousins's choice) becoming his successor.

So the Monday following his weekend resignation from government, Cousins returned to Transport House, causing a small crisis with Harry Nicholas, who was immediately concerned about the future of his office, car and salary. This was all smoothed over, and GEC Chair Len Forden averted a further difficulty by giving up his TUC General Council seat, in order to allow both Cousins and Nicholas to serve. The GEC did, however, order Cousins, against his will, to resign his parliamentary seat as soon as the fight against the incomes legislation was over. So, unlike Bevin's period in office, Cousins's spell in government was not a success, although he left ministerial office with his integrity intact. (The same cannot by any means be said for all trade unionists who have taken up political careers.) He was not tempted by offers to re-enter parliament once he had retired from the T&G.[17]

At the 1966 TUC, now free from the obligations of government, Cousins set out the union's essential position: 'The TGWU believes you cannot have a social democracy and at the same time control by legislation the activity of a free trade union movement which is an essential part of any social democracy'. The arguments around that viewpoint were to dominate the labour movement's politics for a generation.[18]

It was not all criticism, however. The union played a constructive industrial role where it saw the opportunity. For example, it signed a trail-blazing productivity agreement with Esso at its Fawley oil refinery near Southampton, which linked wage increases with higher productivity. The T&G's case was that this was a better deal for the workers and the country than rigid pay 'norms' imposed by government. Union control over incentive payments was key to making the agreement work.[19]

Cousins also began to forge an alliance with Hugh Scanlon, the newly-elected left-wing President of the Engineering Union (the country's second largest), a relationship that was to fully flower under Jack Jones. They shared, among much else, an opposition to state interference in wage negotiations, and collective bargaining more generally. But the T&G view was not simply 'free collective bargaining' and leave it at that. Cousins's view was that:

> there has to be new standards for trade union recognition with the right to set up pay and productivity committees and nationally, there needs to be a rationalisation of national negotiations. Training and re-training has to be revolutionised so that men can be better fitted for the work that has to be done and additional skills created so that they can move from job to job.[20]

In Place of Strife

The T&G's last great struggle of the 1960s, and the last under the leadership of Cousins, was provoked by the government's 'In Place of Strife' legislation, which aimed to bring the law into collective bargaining, including curbing the right to take strike action. The T&G and the rest of the movement strongly objected to the proposed financial penalties (to be deducted directly from wages) for those failing to comply with 'a conciliation pause' or 'cooling off period' before taking industrial action.

'To trade unionists the real issue seems fairly simple,' wrote Frank Cousins in the *T&G Record*:

> The battle for a rising standard of living is part of the struggle between representatives of the workers and management, with the odds almost inevitably on the side of management. Any action in the legislative field is judged by whether this is for one side in the struggle or the other. Most workers will feel that the government is making it even harder to get fair replies to claims

submitted, and must be helping the employers to retain their position of privilege.[21]

The legislation was being promoted by Barbara Castle, hitherto regarded as a left-wing firebrand. According to Jack Jones, she was 'anxious to do things for the workers but not with them. Her outlook was not all that unusual in politicians of the left'.[22]

Opposition to the bill was strongest among the rank-and-file, leading to one of the strongest movement's 'from below' in British trade union history. The Liaison Committee for the Defence of Trade Unions, led by Communist militant Kevin Halpin, took over one million workers out on strike in protest, on May Day 1969. The TUC affirmed its unalterable opposition to the legislation in June, and the penal clauses were finally dropped. This great struggle, however, was only a dress rehearsal for confrontation with the more determined Conservative government that was elected in 1970.[23]

Demonstrating against 'In Place of Strife' 1969

A changing culture

When weighing up the respective contributions of the different eminent leaders of the T&G, one view seems unarguable: no leader *changed* the union more than Cousins. Bevin built it up, of course, and Jones's record of achievement may be greater. But Cousins inherited the T&G in one condition and left it as something very different.

He altered the balance between officials' opinions and members' desires in favour of the latter. He took the union from being a bulwark of Cold War trade unionism and made it a linchpin of progressive politics. He asserted its independence in the industrial sphere at the expense of the conformist doctrine previously prevailing. And he breathed life into its atrophied democracy. None of this was his work alone, but it will all be forever associated with his name.

Cousins began the policy of pushing power downwards and outwards from the centre of the union. Regions gained authority at the expense of national officials and Central Office. He also dealt, albeit belatedly, with the authoritarian holdover of the ban on Communists holding office. He was criticised for postponing the addressing of this issue, including by Bill Jones (no longer a Party member himself). It may be, as Goodman argues, that he felt it was opening up one fight too many with the large number of officials still around who had been raised in the Deakin spirit, particularly in view of his challenge to Labour Party orthodoxy on many other fronts. But at any event, under prodding from Jack Jones (for whom the whole thing 'smelled of McCarthyism'), he finally gave the green light for the ending of the ban, which was by then being ignored in many parts of the union and causing considerable industrial complications where it was still being implemented. In 1968 the GEC agreed to ask that year's Rules Conference to abandon the offensive clause, which it did by an overwhelming majority.[24]

In general, the T&G breathed more easily under the leadership of Cousins, something discernible in small ways as well as large. In

1966, Cousins and a large section of the T&G delegation refused to rise from their seats to join in a standing ovation for Harold Wilson's speech, because of the disagreement over incomes policy. But one third of the union's delegates did get to their feet. Such a public division and defiance of the leader would have been inconceivable under Bevin or Deakin.

His legacy also included giving a lead in tackling the poison of racism, a question which will be explored more fully in the next chapter, and which had already started to raise painful questions for the unions, and the T&G in particular. Cousins was an unabashed champion of race equality and fighting discrimination. In his last speech to a Labour Party conference he said:

> We can win this struggle as we have won so many. It is a struggle against prejudice and for the rights of people. We must work together with the coloured workers if we want to defeat the forces of capitalism and oppression. Let us join together; let us mean it and let them be our brothers.

The language may be dated, but the sentiments are enduring, and they perhaps marked the foundation of the T&G's historic commitment to race equality. And with Cousins it was not just a matter of words – even before leaving the T&G he had taken up part-time office as the first Chairman of the new Community Relations Commission, a position he continued to hold after his retirement.[25]

Cousins's own assessment of his time in office is a fair one. He wrote in *The Sunday Telegraph* shortly before his retirement:

> When I arrived I found a trade union 'establishment' very firmly in control. These people believed absolutely in imposing decisions from the top ... Now thirteen years later much of the apathy that marked official trade unionism has disappeared. There is more freedom, more open-mindedness and ordinary workers are increasingly being encouraged to demand, and to get, a bigger say

in the running of their own unions and the industries in which they work.[26]

Or in Geoffrey Goodman's judgment:

> He ... radicalized and democratized the T&G in a form and with a style that would have been unrecognizable in the period of Bevin and Deakin; he had influenced the entire trade union movement in a profound sense as well as the Labour Party and indeed wider areas of the whole nation. He fought to lift the sights of ordinary people everywhere ... to goals and objectives far beyond the limits of the work-bench and the smokestacks.

Indeed, the growth of working-class aspirations provided the framework for the whole development of trade unionism in the 1950s and 1960s, and the genius of Cousins lay in articulating this change.[27]

John Cousins, a national official of the union in his own right, paid tribute to the enduring political relevance of his father's contribution: 'His opposition to incomes policy, which led him to resign from the Wilson government, and his stand against nuclear weapons, are still relevant today'.[28]

But it was Andy Holmes, Chair of the Irish region of the T&G, who paid perhaps the most quoted tribute to the departing General Secretary: 'Cousins dragged the union from the darkness into the daylight'.[29]

Notes

1. Goodman, p73.
2. Fuller, p224.
3. Jones, p143.
4. Goodman, p114.
5. Hutt, p189; Jones, p143.
6. Fuller, pp226-7; Hutt, p199; Goodman, pp177-199.
7. Jones, p149.
8. Hutt, p211.

9. Goodman, p155.

10. Hutt, p204.

11. Goodman, p282.

12. Hutt, p221; Jones, p160.

13. *T&G Record*, October 1963.

14. Goodman, p367.

15. See Goodman, p471.

16. Goodman 2, p101.

17. Jones, p179, Goodman, p479 ff.

18. Goodman 2, p105.

19. Goodman 2, p113.

20. Goodman 2, p119.

21. *T&G Record*, March 1969.

22. Jones, p193.

23. Hutt, p229.

24. Stevenson, pp43-45; Jones, p133.

25. Goodman 2, p126.

26. Goodman, p584.

27. Goodman 3, p29.

28. Geoffrey Goodman interview.

29. Goodman 3, p12.

6. The world the T&G made 1969–1979

The 1970s was the decade when trade union power in Britain reached its zenith – the years when the T&G's general secretary was widely regarded as the 'most powerful man in the country', when the membership of TUC-affiliated unions passed thirteen million (more than half the workforce) and when the unions were often denounced as a force making the country 'ungovernable'.

As with any summary description of a complex period in history, the handed-down wisdom (written as ever by the victors) includes a large amount of myth. Who now remembers that the British economy actually grew faster on average in the 'grim' 1970s than it did in the rip-roaring Thatcherite 1980s? Who recalls that at a time when the unions could apparently 'hold the country to ransom' and dictate policy to Downing Street, they could not secure recognition at a small north London film processing firm called Grunwick?

In fact, these were the years when the perceptive historian Eric Hobsbawm proposed – controversially at the time – that the 'forward march of labour' had been halted. So it proved, at least for a generation.

But perhaps the greatest myth, and one that flows from a clear class view of life, is that the 1970s were a dismal decade from which we were only redeemed by the Iron Lady and neo-liberal economics. In fact, they were good years for millions of working-class people in that, through their unions, they had achieved a measure of control over the labour process and their interests were recognised (although far from entrenched) in public life. It was a time of improving living standards, generally low (if rising) unemployment, broad social improvements and relatively stable communities. As Ken Gill, leader of the engineering union TASS during the 1970s, puts it:

> When people got sacked, they just got another job. It was great to know that if you went on strike and a factory shut down, you could just get work somewhere else … people go on about the 1970s being a terrible time, but they were a great period for the working class. It was a marvellous time for working people … people were not unhappy. You didn't have the jails full then.[1]

It was, of course, far from ideal, and the strains which were to erupt in the 1980s and beyond were already evident, including within the labour movement itself. But it was a world founded on systematically challenging the twin divine rights – the right of management to manage, and of the ruling class to rule.

And it was a world which the T&G, above all, created.

The Jones philosophy

In the course of the 1970s the T&G became the largest trade union organisation in the capitalist world, peaking at over two million members by the end of the decade. It was certainly the most powerful democratic working-class organisation in Britain's history, and it was, more than at any previous period in its own development, reflective of the views, attitudes and outlook of those members. This was the product of the struggles of the 1950s and 1960s, as already described, but it was also very much the result of the philosophy of Jack Jones. For the T&G, the 1970s began in September 1969, when Jones succeeded Frank Cousins as General Secretary. As Cousins had hoped, Jones prevailed easily in the ballot for the post, winning over 334,000 votes, with the nearest of the ten other candidates gaining a mere 28,000.

What was the Jones philosophy? In his own words: 'I did all I could to make it an effective trade union rather than a union that was inclined to ... appease the big employers.' Members first, decentralise authority while setting clear national objectives for improvements, promote socialist values and run a disciplined organisation. Building on the Cousins legacy in all these respects, Jones established the T&G as unarguably the century's most important trade union and himself as, more arguably, the most important trade unionist.[2]

Jack Jones was born in Liverpool in 1913. He left school at 14 and worked as a docker in the port, where he began his trade union life – frequently in conflict with local T&G officialdom. He famously served with the International Brigades in the Spanish Civil War and was wounded at the Battle of Ebro. On his return he became a full-time official of the T&G in Coventry and helped to keep the city's munitions industry working through the great wartime destruction, at the same time building the T&G's strength in the factories by leaps and bounds. After the war he served in a variety of positions in the Midlands region, organising the work force in the car and engineering industries and eventually becoming Regional Secretary. Jones was a firm supporter of Cousins's new course from the outset, and, after moving to London as number three in the T&G hierarchy, was in the front-line of trying to make the T&G more responsive to its membership and more militant towards employers.

Within the union, Jones showed his commitment to the Cousins approach in his determination to decentralise authority, to push power down to the districts and to base the union on a strong shop stewards network. Drawing on his memories of Deakinism, Jones determined 'to do all in my power to ensure that no agreement was concluded without the knowledge and approval of the membership'.[3]

Shop stewards were the key to his structure and strategy: 'The membership ... had to be able to elect their spokesmen at the point of production, the point of operation. Then you built from there upwards ... you had to develop the collective participation, collective voice'.[4]

Power to the membership was matched by a more demanding approach towards the work of full-time officials. Some national officers had been heard defining their role as being 'half-way between the members and the management'. A number 'still tended to side with the employers rather than our members'. Emphasising recruitment and organisation, Jones 'insisted that each full-time officer must be made accountable for his results'.[5]

This demanding approach to full-time officers produced its casualties, even before Jones became the union's leader. For example, in 1966 a crisis erupted in Hull docks. Members were pouring out of the union, and efforts to address men's complaints were being met with obstruction from the three full-time officers, who were dismissed after an investigation headed by Jones. As he commented later, 'The Hull experience only sharpened my determination to bring about more democracy in the union, with every official responsible to an elected committee within his area of operation'.[6] Jones also recalled in his book that 'more than one national official left the service of the union in a hurry. One officer claimed expenses for an engagement in Dublin. Since I knew he had no business there I challenged him, only to be told lamely that "he'd been on a secret mission"'!

It was in the 1970s that the T&G's cherished tradition of lay democracy – of officials really answering to the members they served – started to take a firmer hold. Partly that was, no doubt, a consequence of a generational change, as the officials appointed under Bevin and Deakin began to leave the service of the union, removing the obstacle which Cousins had found such an encumbrance. But it was also because of the leadership that came from the top, and the conviction shared by Jones and his number two Harry Urwin that a two million-strong working-class organisation could not be effectively run as an autocracy. The removal of the ban on Communist Party members holding office also contributed to the growing strength of the Broad Left, which increasingly came to set the union's political course, and influence the appointment of a new generation of full-time officials.[7]

Battles in the car industry

The storm centre of trade unionism in the 1960s and 1970s, at least in the public mind, was the motor industry, largely because of the frequency of unofficial strikes in the huge factories at its core. In the T&G the big car plants – mostly owned by giant global monopolies – began to assume the role as centres of militancy that had in earlier generations been played by the docks and the buses. Car workers were consistently reviled in the media in those years, by people with no understanding of the harsh realities of work in the factories. Bernie Passingham, a long-standing shop steward at Ford's Dagenham plant, describes life on the assembly line:

> Working on the line was filthy, dirty and noisy. Basically you had to have a bath every night. The metal dust that was flying around would turn your underclothes rusty … but what really caused the trouble was the speed-up. We used to have a works standard man come round, and he'd time you with his watch. Then the foreman would come and say 'well, you've got to produce faster'. But it just didn't work out like that, because you felt you were working and sweating hard enough as it was. You were given so many seconds to do this, and so many seconds to do that, and it didn't go down well with the workers. They were constantly cracking the whip and trying to get more and more out of us. Well, that annual time study caused lots of disputes and strikes.[8]

Tony Woodley, later T&G general secretary, started as a teenager in the Ellesmere Port plant of Vauxhall, British subsidiary of General Motors, then the largest business in the world:

It was a difficult industry built on conflict with the gaffer, the employer equally determined to beat down the trade unions ... I can remember in Vauxhalls we had to go on strike for five weeks just to get a guaranteed shift, because for every single week in the whole year, we didn't get a weekend.

Through no fault of our own the gaffer laid us off, they orchestrated a dispute, or they decided they had a part missing. We would come in on nights for example, having slept all day, and at eleven o'clock the tannoy would go 'you are now laid off – please come in tomorrow we may have work'. Just like that, no consideration that you couldn't sleep, that you'd lost a fifth of your pay for that week or maybe more ... We had to battle for everything. It was very rough, it was very tough, it was antagonistic and brutal, but it was a massive learning curve for people like me.[9]

Gradually the unions made progress in introducing elements of civilisation into this process. Passingham again:

you had stoppages at work – you used to stop the line and you used to lose, what, hundreds of cars – coming down [the line] was fifty cars an hour. Slowly and surely industrial relations came round, and the thinking, so there got to be more consultation with the workers ... with the shop stewards ... they started giving the convenor an office ... slowly but slowly it came to the point where you weren't just battling against a brick wall.[10]

Increasingly, the motor and engineering industries became central to the T&G, accounting for a large and growing proportion of the membership and bringing the factory culture to the heart of the union. Workers shaped in the industry, like Ron Todd (Ford Dagenham), Jack Adams (British Leyland Longbridge) and Tony Woodley (Vauxhall Ellesmere Port), came to play a decisive part in the balance of the T&G's history.

Jack Jones speaks

Car industry conflict: Ford workers hail Moss Evans

Ford sewing machinists go into action

The car industry was also the setting for one of the most emblematic disputes of the era – the Ford sewing machinists strike. This took place in 1968, shortly before the dawn of the 'Jones era', but its ramifications were felt industrially and politically in the 1970s. Women sewing machinists at the company's Dagenham plant took strike action in support of a claim for parity with similarly-skilled men in the 'C' grade. After three weeks on a strike which shut down the whole vast plant, they settled for 92 per cent of the C grade rate. The dispute was given an even higher profile when Barbara Castle, then Employment Minister, stepped in to help negotiate the settlement.

Dora Challingworth, one of the women who led the strike, recalls:

> The women wanted not only equal pay, they wanted equality – the job they did wasn't classed as skilled and they wanted their skills recognised ... the men who cut the work got C grade, and the women were B grade, and we had to put it all together. I mean, they only cut it by stencil, which in our eyes was easy, but we had nothing to follow, we were just given the parts and you had to figure it out ... it was hard work, because a lot of it was like PVC, and the leather at the time was really hard ... I had to have an operation on my hands, through the actual pulling of the work.[11]

Bernie Passingham, who as a shop steward supported the machinists, drew on the lessons of the previous decade of progressive change within the T&G when he was negotiating a settlement: 'Leslie Blayton, industrial relations manager at Fords, was at Barbara Castle's office ... and he says "what do you want to settle it?", and all I said was "equal pay" ... because that had been driven into me by Frank Cousins and Jack Jones.'[12]

The strike led to great changes in the attitude towards working women and their rights. As current TUC deputy general secretary

Frances O'Grady has pointed out, 'we wouldn't have the Equal Pay Act without the Ford sewing machinists' strike action'.[13]

However, it cannot be said that the T&G immediately adapted to the growing importance of women in the workforce, and the increasing necessity of reflecting that fact in the policies, structures and attitudes of the trade unions. Margaret Prosser, later the union's deputy general secretary, recalls as a struggle her own early days in the T&G, in the 1970s: 'The whole emphasis of the union was nothing to do with us … women were a bit on the edge. They certainly weren't central to anything and weren't important in anyone's eyes … our bread and butter membership was in the big factories, very male dominated – or the docks of course and transport.'

When Prosser was later appointed as a full-time officer, some of the members were 'most astonished that they had a woman officer, because there hadn't been a woman industrial officer in the union in the southeast of England for donkey's years'. There was even a

Ford sewing machinists strike for equality

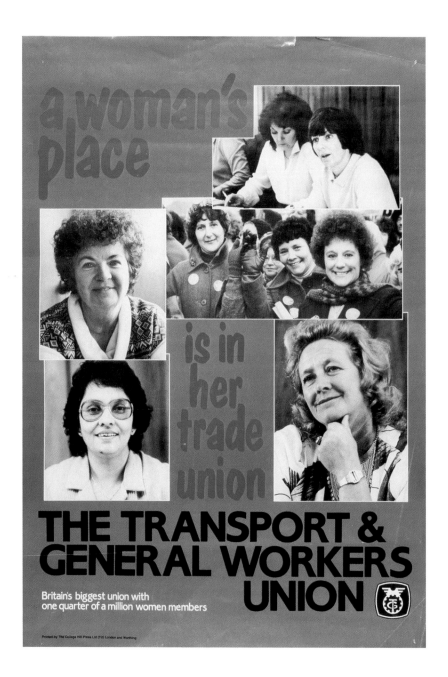

A women's place

suggestion that a man be appointed to the job of national women's officer when the post became vacant, an idea that was only dropped when it was realised that a man would be ineligible to take up the women's seat on the TUC General Council that had been held by the previous incumbent.

Prosser recalled receiving a letter from a woman who worked in the offices of a coach building company in West London, and wanted to work part-time

> the union official wouldn't hear of this, wouldn't have any negotiations about her going part-time. So on her behalf I wrote what I thought was a fairly polite letter … and he wrote me the most shirty letter back; the union wasn't interested in part-timers, he said – this is a union for coach builders, you know.[14]

Changing that sort of attitude was to take a generation of struggle within the T&G, much of it conducted by Prosser herself; and it remains unfinished business, despite the considerable progress that was made later.

Race equality in the union

The other major change in the workforce was the rapid growth in the numbers of black workers, both men and women. These workers were part of the postwar wave of immigration from the West Indies and South Asia, in the 1950s and 1960s – and, later, the first generation of their British-born descendants.

Immigrant labour had started to impact on the T&G in the 1950s. London Buses had been one of the industries specially targeted by the government for the recruitment of workers from the West Indies, in the hope of finding a source of cheaper labour. There were initial fears in the workforce about wages and conditions being undermined, but these were to a considerable degree overcome within the union after the 1958 strike. One conductor said: 'they stuck by the union in the big strike, although no-one expected them to. It was OK after that'.[17]

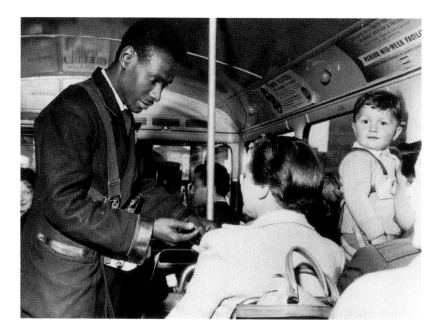

Many industries began to rely on black workers in the postwar period.

However, anti-immigrant attitudes did persist among a section of the membership. Trevor Carter, a historian of Afro-Caribbean involvement in the labour movement, has documented 'one-day strikes by Transport and General Workers Union members against the employment of black transport workers'. (But he has also identified occasions when disputes about entirely unrelated questions were misrepresented in the media as being about immigrant labour.)[16]

In general, the labour movement did not hasten to address the problems faced by black workers. It was torn between its traditions of solidarity and the feeling that immigration was unpopular in many working-class communities. The Wilson government eventually passed legislation against race discrimination, although the TUC's Vic Feather opposed the move.[17]

It was Enoch Powell who dramatically brought these issues to the centre of the public agenda in 1968. In a notorious racist speech he forecast 'rivers of blood' flowing in Britain unless immigration was halted and reversed (notwithstanding that he had been Health

Minister in the Macmillan government when such immigration had been actively promoted to assist in NHS staffing). His lurid address, peppered with unsubstantiated and exaggerated anecdotes, was an incitement to an escalation of racial tension. His speech was particularly popular among two sections of the T&G's London membership – dockers and porters at the Smithfield meat market.

It is almost certainly not coincidental that the London docks and markets had an entirely white workforce at the time, unlike many other T&G-organised industries. And it is certainly the case that only a minority of either group took part in the public demonstrations in support of Powell – which were, of course, widely promoted in a press eager to play up Powell's views and the degree of public support for them. Nevertheless, when a fellow docker pointed out to his colleagues expressing backing for Powell outside Parliament that their hero was a Tory, he was met with shouted responses: 'he's English' and 'he's white'. Here one can see some of the incipient fault lines that were eventually to nourish Thatcherism.

A leading T&G activist in the docks, Mick Connolly, emphasises that this expression of support was only the work of a minority.

> We were talking about a group of no more than two hundred dockworkers who were fairly vocal ... we do know that in Smithfield Market there was an element of the National Front, which was the predominant fascist organisation of the time ... There was never at that time or subsequently any real fascist organisation among dockers in London ... it was not typical of working dockers, it certainly wasn't typical of workers in London more generally, and it was a very short run campaign.

Connolly attributes the incident more to the effect of the changes sweeping docklands at the time:

> It was a strange enclosed industry ... it was very much at the time dads and lads, and you went into the industry via your father. It

was very much built around communities. When you started to see some of the enclosed docks in London closing I suppose the impact would be like a pit closure in a very urban environment ... so there were fears about real communities starting to erode.[18]

Jack Jones also downplays the significance of these manifestations of racism within the union, but he is clear that it represented the visible portion of a much larger problem:

I was shocked by the march of a couple of hundred dockers from the East End to express support for Powell. A couple of hundred out of over 21,000 registered dockers in the Port of London was not much, but it was a straw in the wind ... I had heard influential trade union leaders expressing sympathy for Powell's views. In the ranks of trade unionism racial feelings were ablaze, fanned by the winds of ignorance and prejudice ... racialist attitudes had to be fought, even if this meant unpopularity.[19]

There was no doubt where Cousins and Jones stood on this issue. As already noted, the former gave over much of his time in his first years of retirement to promoting good race relations. They stood in the tradition of solidarity against any form of racism, which they saw as an instrument of the capitalists. However, it would be naïve to suppose that these views informed the entirety of the union's work at the time. For example, there are too many instances of unions collaborating in the herding of Pakistani and Bengali workers onto the night-shift in the textile mills of the north or the foundries of the Black Country. Despite the adoption of anti-racist policies, which put the trade union movement ahead of much of society, unions were slow to convert this positive outlook into real changes in their own practice and procedures.

As a coda to the Powell episode it should be noted that when Bill Morris stood for election in 1991, to become British trade unionism's first black leader, the London dockers (by then much diminished in numbers of course) were among his strongest supporters.

Challenging Heath

The early 1970s saw the industrial struggle in Britain at its sharpest level since the years immediately after World War One. The situation was similar across much of western Europe. One underlying reason was increasing working-class confidence, born of years of almost-full employment and extending self-organisation – allied to the frustration that had built up over years of productivity increases that were only partly reflected in wages. Governments were more and more turning to inflation as an instrument to reduce real incomes. This was a convenient tool since, unpopular as inflation was with almost all classes, its persistence could nevertheless be blamed on the wage demands of 'greedy unions', though in fact these seldom aimed higher than the protection of the real value of members' incomes. Had employers directly cut money wages, as would have happened in earlier times, this fiction could not have been maintained.

Successive governments sought a way to undermine the ability of the working class to protect its living standards. Labour and Tory alike were confronted with the reality of a powerful trade union movement that could not easily be defeated through confrontation. They were also politically hamstrung by the commitment to the maintenance of full employment, which had become embedded as part of the post-war political consensus. Allowing a rapid rise in unemployment would, of course, have been the easiest way of undermining the position of the trade unions, but this was still held to be politically suicidal and socially dangerous in the early 1970s.

Behind all this lurked a still more fundamental issue – the 'who's in charge here' question. The rise in the strength of the organised working class, and the measure of control over the labour process established in many industries, challenged the natural order of things in the eyes of the establishment and industry's management. The idea of the country becoming 'ungovernable' actually meant 'harder to govern by those born to govern in the way they wanted to govern it'. The mass media became infected with an increasingly strident and neurotic anti-trade unionism. The view of the eminent academic AL Rowse – that British workers were guilty of 'brute selfishness and bloody-mindedness, forever striking' – became the public orthodoxy of the time, in defiance of all evidence and reason.[20]

Wilson's failed 'In Place of Strife' proposals represented the first crack at resolving these problems in the interests of capitalism. For the next ten years, government wavered between trying to kill union power by coercion or doing it by co-option. The Tory administration headed by Edward Heath from 1970 to 1974 adopted both approaches during its time in office. Initially setting off in a direction which would later be termed 'Thatcherite', Heath introduced an Industrial Relations Act, which included the setting up of a National Industrial Relations Court with powers to punish trade unions for taking industrial action. The T&G, along with the rest of the movement, determined not to co-operate with the Act and demanded its repeal.

When the London dockers started picketing container depots (to stop their work being transferred there), the National Industrial Relations Court fined the union an eventual total of £55,000. 'This disastrous anti-trade union legislation, which is now recognised as being clearly responsible for creating industrial chaos, must go,' wrote Jack Jones in the *T&G Record*.

A second court order, relating to picketing at another container firm, led to five dockers being jailed in London's Pentonville prison. 'One in the Dock, All Out the Docks' was the slogan in the Port of London. The TUC decided to call a one-day general strike if the men were not released, under pressure from the Liaison Committee for Defence of Trade Unions, which had stated it would itself call a strike if Congress House did not act.

At this point, the government took fright and discovered an obscure functionary known as the Official Solicitor, who ordered the men's release on a technicality. The five then emerged from Pentonville to a hero's welcome. 'The dockers were released and carried shoulder

Pentonville Five: Vic Turner is sprung from jail

high in a victory march through the streets of London. This lightning action was one of the finest episodes in British trade union history,' wrote Allen Hutt.[21]

T&G member Vic Turner was one of the five: 'I was amazed at the amount of public support that we got and it showed me that the British public will always rise when they think there's an injustice taking place.'

Reflecting on all this 36 years later, Turner explained the attitudes which informed his stand at the time:

I have said to younger people 'unless you're prepared to stand up and be counted to defend not just your industry but your whole way of life and your whole culture, then you're not a member of the working class.' And that's the way I put it … but to ask people to break the law. I would do it. I wouldn't ask other people to do it, you know, but … it's a defence of what your parents and grandparents have striven for.

At the time the employer's attitude was 'there it is, that's all your getting, that's it. Don't wanna talk to you no more, get out of here' … so that's what made your reaction.

The trade unions are more important than the Labour government … because a trade union will defend you from the cradle to the grave. That's their role in life. You can't say that of Labour or any other government … The membership only get the sort of trade union they deserve … I would never have felt right when I was at work, if I didn't attend my branch and make my contribution and support my fellow workers irrespective.[22]

The 'Pentonville Five' confrontation was only one of many marking the industrial landscape of the early 1970s. In 1972 the miners went on national strike for the first time since 1926, winning a considerable pay increase after a dispute marked by the widespread use of secondary picketing. In Glasgow, the workforce of Upper Clyde Shipbuilders occupied their yards – again successfully – to prevent closure. These were bold assertions of working-class self-confidence, with the potential to move beyond the normal bounds of industrial action.

Militancy also brought results for the dockers. A strike brought an end to the temporary unattached register, a further step towards an end to casualisation. All registered dockers were now to be given permanent employment on pay of more than £50 a week (a very large sum for the time), with a generous voluntary severance scheme to deal with the problems being caused by containerisation. The package was only agreed after the noisy and divided conference that accompanied most transactions of important business for the docks group. After Jones had succeeded in persuading the membership of the benefits of the deal he had negotiated:

> one of the shop stewards from the London Docks came up to me. He was holding his little son by the hand. 'What about my future?' he asked. 'You've got a permanent job as a result of this agreement,' I replied. 'Ah,' he said, 'but what about the boy?'[23]

In the face of this mass militancy, Heath began to retreat. Jones writes that TUC general secretary Vic Feather 'was attracted to establishment figures like a moth to a candle', and began to cultivate the Prime Minister, while the T&G leader himself confessed that he 'found it was easier to chat with [Heath] than with some Labour friends like Roy Jenkins'. However, this availed the Tory leader nothing, as he was voted out of office in February 1974 in the midst of a second miners' strike. He had asked the electorate to determine 'who governs Britain?' and the voters took the view that if the Prime Minister didn't know then it shouldn't be him. Harold Wilson returned to Downing Street.[24]

The T&G in Ireland

The story of the T&G in Ireland, in both the north and the Republic, is to some extent a story in itself, separate from many of the industrial and most of the political narratives which defined the union in Great Britain. This was highlighted during the Spanish Civil War, when the Amalgamated T&GWU (as the union was known in Ireland to distinguish it from the larger and entirely separate Irish T&GWU founded by Connolly and Larkin) was the only union to come out in support of the Republican side. This was too much for some branches in what was then the clerical-dominated and hence pro-Franco Free State, which seceded from the union in protest!

The union's Irish region always enjoyed considerable latitude in the conduct of its business, reflecting this different history. Indeed, it had to represent a considerable membership in the separate – and increasingly distinct – jurisdiction of the Republic of Ireland. While the union membership in the huge Belfast workplaces of Shorts and Harland and Woolf – both in public ownership in the 1970s – were closely connected to their colleagues in Britain, they also faced unique difficulties arising from the political and sectarian crises which marked life in Northern Ireland and entirely engulfed it from 1969 onwards.

The crisis which erupted from the brutal assaults on the civil rights movement by Stormont's police and special forces, and led in short order to the dispatch of the British Army to Northern Ireland in strength, posed a special challenge to the trade union movement. It is no exaggeration to say that it was the main bastion of a non-sectarian approach to the problems in the six counties, endeavouring to bind people together at work even as almost every other factor in play in the community was driving them apart. A leading part was played by the AT&GWU and successive regional secretaries in this work, which balanced a progressive approach to addressing the huge social and economic problems in the region with the need to refrain from positions which would split the working class and the union wide apart.

A mighty union

With the return of Labour government, the T&G reached the apogee of its influence on British life. It was by any measure a mighty industrial machine in the mid-1970s. The 1.5 million member mark had been passed in 1969, but that was only a way-station. In the next three years of intense industrial struggle, the union added a further 250,000 members. All over the country working men and women were organising themselves and finding a natural home in the T&G, spreading as it did over so many sectors of the economy. The membership profile of the union was also changing. While most people still saw the T&G as a union for dockers, bus and lorry drivers and car workers, it was now growing rapidly in the public services, civil aviation and other white-collar sections, including the voluntary sector.

And the dynamic, progressive image of the T&G once more proved a magnet to other unions seeking amalgamation. The Plasterers Union, 'a craft union which had played a great part in the history of the building industry', according to Jones, merged with the T&G in 1969.[25]

The amalgamation with the Scottish Commercial Motormen's Union, who included among their number Alex Kitson (a future T&G deputy general secretary), strengthened the union in the road haulage sector; and the merger with the Chemical Workers Union, led by Bob Edwards MP, boosted the T&G in that major industry. Several mergers consolidated the T&G position in the docks,

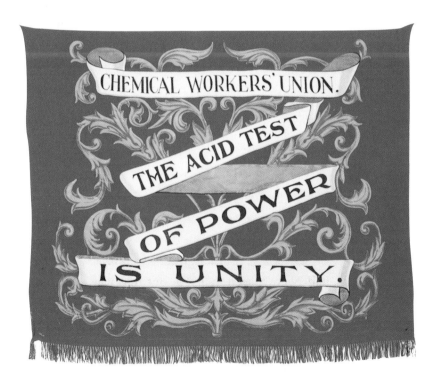

The Chemical Workers merge with the T&G

transforming it from being the major union – for most purposes in most major ports – to become the only one. The Scottish TGWU (Docks) finally ended the split in Glasgow by merging in 1972, while the Lightermen's Union in London also came in, leaving only the stevedores union outside, for a little longer.

In the centrally important motor industry, the National Union of Vehicle Builders, originally founded in the early nineteenth century and a repository of craft traditions, also came on board in 1972. Led by Alf Roberts and Grenville Hawley, it included amongst its members a young Tony Woodley, who would be elected as the T&G's general secretary more than thirty years later.

In September 1977, T&G membership passed the two million mark, a figure not reached in Britain either before or since by any union. As Jones remarked:

> It was not for me the magic of numbers but the growing popularity of the union in the workplace which mattered. More and more people were coming to rely on the weapon of trade unionism as represented by the T&G.

The union was also deepening its links with its own membership. Jones revamped the *T&G Record* as a popular tabloid-style newspaper, blazing a trail for other union journals and greatly increasing its appeal. And he organised the building of a large convalescent and residential centre at Eastbourne, a facility which remains busy to this day.

Not all aspects of his vision were realised however. Jones backed the proposals of the Bullock Commission for worker-directors throughout industry, but these fizzled out amidst opposition in the political arena, from both the left and right. Nor did the T&G prevail in the referendum on continued membership of the EEC. Jones campaigned vigorously for a 'no' vote, which was popular with trade unionists because of the EEC's impact in raising the cost of living and putting employment at risk. He even – somewhat against his better judgement – shared a platform with Enoch Powell in the course of the campaign.

In the face of the united pro-EEC position of the two front benches in parliament, however, the 'No' campaign was heavily defeated.

It is important to understand that the trade unions were far from being all powerful in the 1970s. The story of Grunwick is well-known. The trade unions were unable to win union recognition for the mainly Asian female workforce in the face of an intransigent employer enjoying full backing from the Tory Party, despite a long campaign of mass picketing in which Jack Dromey, later to become T&G deputy general secretary, was heavily involved.

The long occupation of the Imperial Typewriters factory at Hull in 1975 was another example of the limitations as well as the potential of trade union power, and (unlike Grunwick) it was a

International solidarity: Deputy general secretary
Alex Kitson greets Isabel Allende

dispute in which the T&G was directly involved. Val Burn, later a T&G executive member, was one of the women at the forefront of this struggle:

> we'd finished our day's work, I'd gone home, I was preparing the tea and my telephone started ringing ... it was members who worked at Imperial typewriters to say they'd received this letter, we were no longer to return to Imperial, they'd closed down and we would receive a further letter telling us when we would be allowed back in to pick up our belongings ... So, we all decided we would arrive at the gate at six o'clock in the morning, which was the time many of us went for shift work ... and all of a sudden somebody shouted 'right, over we go' and three hundred of us went over the gates.[26]

And so began one of the longest factory occupations against closure in British history. It lasted for six months, with women maintaining the occupation during the day, and the men at night, 'because people would try and make mischief'. On the first day the Hull dockers turned up at the gates with a solidarity gift of three hundred portions of fish and chips. The sit-in finally ended under threat of court injunctions from the employer that could have cost the workers their homes. Tony Benn, Secretary of State for Industry at the time, recalls: 'where the interests of the trade unions conflicted with capital, the Treasury and my own officials were always working with capital against the trade unions – Imperial Typewriters is a good example.' The realities of class power were shaken, but not transformed, in the 1970s.[27]

Debates on the Social Contract

The return of Labour to office meant no abatement in struggle: days lost to strike action remained high throughout the decade. However, the political relationship between unions and government altered. Labour took over in an atmosphere of national and international economic crisis, highlighted by the quadrupling of the price of oil in the wake of the 1973 Middle East war. 'Fighting inflation' was Labour's top priority, and the negotiation of a 'social contract' with the unions was the central initiative taken by ministers to that end.[28]

Under its provisions, a tight regime of wage restraint, binding on everyone, was imposed – at either a fixed percentage or a flat rate from one year to the next – and in return union interests were to be reflected in the passage of sympathetic legislation and in consultation over economic management. Right from the start, the left in the unions opposed the Social Contract, on the grounds that it meant the abandonment of free collective bargaining and represented an attempt to damp down the level of working-class combativeness, the better to make workers bear the burden of resolving the economic crisis. A counter-critique from a minority of the left argued that an incomes policy was an important means of tackling inequality, particularly for women and other low-paid workers, and that free collective bargaining was of most use to the already stronger sections of the working class.

These arguments came to dominate debates within the TUC and the T&G as the decade wore on. They became more acute after the government embarked on radical public spending reductions under pressure from the International Monetary Fund and the City in 1976, which left the ministerial end of the 'contract' looking more than a little threadbare. The problems were exacerbated when Prime Minister James Callaghan (who succeeded Wilson in 1976) and Chancellor Denis Healey sought to extend wage restraint and block any return to free collective bargaining almost indefinitely, ignoring the tensions building up after several years of a wages squeeze.

Jack Jones was without doubt the leading architect of the Social Contract from the trade union side. He was closely consulted by ministers at every step of the way, and was not backward in leveraging the situation for such advantage as he could secure for T&G members and trade unionists more generally. It was in this period that he was dubbed 'the most powerful man in Britain' – an exaggeration to be sure, but a reflection of the power of his union at the time.

His own view of the Social Contract was clear:

> I never doubted the value of the Social Contract, which I saw as a major step towards economic equality and better conditions for working people, and used every democratic means to gain the co-operation of fellow trade unionists. Sometimes I felt that political leaders did not appreciate the hard work involved in influencing rank-and-file opinion.[29]

Certainly, this position moved some way away from that of Cousins and his rock-ribbed commitment to free collective bargaining. However, the 'social contract' was voluntary and not backed by the penal sanctions proposed by Wilson in 1969 and Heath in 1971. And account had to be taken of the precariousness of the political situation, with Labour enjoying nothing like the majority it had in the late 1960s. Initially, Jones was successful in winning the T&G to his view, despite its powerful left wing. The 1975 Biennial Delegate Conference supported the scheme, including the proposal for a levelling flat-rate pay increase for the year ahead. Jones told the Scottish TUC that year:

> My appeal is to respect the Social Contract, and to support it. To do this would mean advancing the interests of our members and keeping a Labour government in power. Can we really afford to let this government be thrown out? The Labour government, for all its limitations, is two hundred times better than a Tory government.[30]

But after the IMF-ordered retreat, the struggle became harder – both with ministers demanding greater sacrifices from the unions with less to offer in return, and with a rank-and-file seeing little gain from the restraint being asked of them. Jones still hoped for a comprehensive deal:

> I knew that Michael Foot and Tony Benn were ready to resign at the drop of a hat, but urged them to remain in the government. We had been promised higher food subsidies, increased grants to keep

council house rents down and other action on prices, as well as measures to reduce unemployment, and it was essential to keep friends in the Cabinet to see such promises were kept.[31]

However, the political context was becoming increasingly alarming, as Labour lost its majority in the House of Commons, becoming dependent on the Liberal Party to stay in office. Meanwhile, Mrs Thatcher had assumed the leadership of the Tory Party, with a hard-right programme. Jones was not alone in seeing the ghosts of 1931 abroad, warning the union that 'the MacDonalds, the Snowdens, the Jimmy Thomases are lurking around ... some of them, including a few in high places, are ready to stick a dagger in the heart of the Labour government'. Indeed, it was his view that 'the majority of the TUC General Council were more loyal to the government than some of its own ministers'.[32]

Under these circumstances the situation gradually began to slip away from the T&G leadership. A Dock Work Regulation Bill, designed to mitigate the effects of containerisation and the development of ports not covered by the Dock Labour Scheme, which were threatening the return of casualisation, was sabotaged by two Labour MPs in the Commons working hand-in-glove with the employers. And unemployment started to rise again, in a sustained way that had not been seen since the end of the war. 'Efforts to keep open factories and other workplaces became my main preoccupation,' Jones wrote. This preoccupation has remained ever since for his successors in the T&G and workers in almost every private sector trade union.[33]

So it was that at the 1977 BDC on the Isle of Man, Jones's last as general secretary, the Executive was defeated in seeking to secure support for continued wage restraint. Delegates instead voted for 'a return to unfettered collective bargaining', despite this warning from Jones in his final major address to his union:

The benefits of North Sea oil and an improved balance of payments are on the horizon. If this government fails you will hand these to

the party of privilege. You will put back the mighty in their seats
and kick the people of low degree in the teeth. That is the danger …

It was a danger which did indeed come to pass, and the extent of the
kicking in the teeth exceeded the worst fears of anyone in the
movement – although many were to argue that it was the policies of
wage restraint, rather than their abandonment, which led to this
disaster.[34]

The Jones legacy

Jack Jones retired from office in 1978, shortly before his worst fears
started to come to pass. He then embarked on what amounted to a
fresh career as a leading champion of pensioners, working through
both the T&G's Retired Members Association and the National
Pensioners Convention to win a better deal for the nation's elderly –
particularly the working-class elderly struggling to survive on the
pittance of a state pension.

He cast a long shadow over the T&G for the rest of its history.
TUC Deputy General Secretary Frances O'Grady, who worked
with Jones on pensioners' issues whilst she was employed at the
T&G, describes him as 'the best Prime Minister we never had …
one of the most creative leaders that we've ever had, one of the most
genuinely intelligent leaders the whole movement has had'.[35]

The idea of Jones being Prime Minister – even though, unlike
Cousins, he had never felt the tug of political office at all – was
widely shared. When he retired from the T&G, the *Daily Mail*
carried a cartoon which showed the actual premier, James
Callaghan, telling his wife that 'Jack Jones has retired' – to which
Audrey replied: '(gulp) Does that mean a general election?'.

Such was the influence of the T&G at the time. The union's
strength and standing by 1978 exceeded, by all measures save the
most important, all the hopes of its founders. The significant
exception was that 'the master class', as Bevin would have styled it
in 1922, was still in power – and viewing the strength of trade

unionism with considerable alarm. Could the 1970s have had a different outcome with a more left-wing leadership of the movement, as has often been argued? Counter-factual history is irresistibly entertaining, but by its nature it can provide no definitive answers. What seems indisputable, however, is that at the moment when the movement that Jack Jones had played such a central part in building was reaching the peak of its strength, support for the socialist ideas for which he was so passionate an advocate was ebbing away, within the working class and beyond. In short, the trade union movement was powerful enough to make it difficult for capitalism to carry on as it wanted, but not powerful enough to replace it altogether, even had it wished to.

Jones himself had few illusions that the gains the T&G had won were secure. Accepting the union's Gold Medal from its Chair Stan Pemberton, a fellow Liverpudlian, he emphasised the need to 'continue organising the unorganised. Organise, that's still a magic word, because with organisation you can move mountains.' It may have seemed an unnecessary lesson when the union had well over two million members, but it was of enduring importance – all the more so for being largely neglected over the next twenty-five years.[36]

The Winter of Discontent

At the height of its power as the T&G was, industrial events were nevertheless moving beyond its control as Jones handed over to his successor Moss Evans, the union's sixth general secretary.

Evans was born in South Wales in 1925, moving to Birmingham at the age of 12, where he joined the AEU while working for Joseph Lucas. His involvement with the T&G started in 1950 when he moved to the Bakelite Factory. He rose from being a shop steward to become a full-time officer in the engineering and chemical trade groups in Birmingham and later London. He was appointed national secretary for the motor industry in 1969 and national organiser four years later. Running from the left, Evans was elected general secretary

Moss Evans rallies the movement

Jack Jones, defiant

in 1978. Frank Cousins's son John was the runner-up among the fourteen other candidates.

Evans inherited a political and industrial situation reaching boiling point. Despite collapsing support for pay restraint in the trade union movement, Callaghan and Healey unwisely decided to seek a further extension of their incomes policy. Callaghan also decided against calling a General Election in the autumn of 1978, when opinion polls suggested he might have won.

Instead, the country plunged into the now-notorious 'winter of discontent'. In fact, the winter of 1978-79 is now as much a season of myths as of anything else. Jim Callaghan never said 'Crisis? What Crisis?', and only one family had to postpone a funeral because of the gravediggers' strike in Liverpool. Society, which had only recently taken Heath's three-day week in its stride, did not collapse. However, the headlines were dominated by a series of conflicts between a government that seemed to have lost any sense of purpose and a trade union movement itself uncertain as to where it was headed. The abiding iconography of the winter was the uncollected rubbish piled high in public spaces in London as a result of a strike by refuse collectors. More significant, perhaps, was the dispute of motor industry toolmakers in the Midlands (AUEW members), eager to restore their craft differentials. This highlighted the divisions opening up in the trade union movement, exacerbated by the abandonment of free collective bargaining – divisions which the Tories were able to play on. West Midlands seats swung decisively towards the Conservatives in 1979, as many trade unionists abandoned Labour at the ballot box for the first time in their lives.

Many sections of the T&G membership were caught up in the action. Ford workers took strike action for a pay-policy-busting wage increase. Lorry drivers also struck, and dockers were involved. Indeed, one Tory MP complained in the Commons that power in Salford had passed into the hands of a 'soviet' consisting of a strike committee at the docks entrance. The charge is at once absurdly inflated but also redolent of the real fears of the establishment at the time, fears which they were able to use to mobilise large sections of public opinion behind a strategy of all-out assault on trade union power. This assault began as the 'winter of discontent' gave way to the springtime of Thatcherism in 1979.

Notes

1. Murray, pp40-41.
2. Geoffrey Goodman interview.
3. Jones, p106.
4. Geoffrey Goodman interview.
5. Jones, pp155, 161.
6. Jones, pp182-83.
7. Jones, p201.
8. Weightman, p346.
9. Geoffrey Goodman interview.
10. Geoffrey Goodman interview.
11. Geoffrey Goodman interview.
12. Geoffrey Goodman interview.
13. Geoffrey Goodman interview.
14. Geoffrey Goodman interview.
15. Fuller, p207.
16. Carter, pp25, 51.
17. Jones, p198.
18. Jack Amos, interview.
19. Jones, p197.
20. Jones, p327.
21. Hutt, pp239-40.
22. Geoffrey Goodman interview.
23. Jones, pp252-53.
24. Jones, pp215, 234.
25. Jones, p194.
26. Geoffrey Goodman interview.
27. Geoffrey Goodman interview.
28. Frieden, p367.
29. Jones, p295.
30. Jones, p295.
31. Jones, p298.
32. Jones, pp300, 309.
33. Jones, pp310-11.
34. Jones, pp325-26.
35. Geoffrey Goodman interview.
36. Jones, p337.

7. The T&G world unmade 1979-2003

The Thatcher offensive

Had the T&G story stopped in 1979, this work would have a happier ending for trade unionists. In fact, the twenty years following Mrs Thatcher's first election as Prime Minister shattered much of the industrial and social position the union had achieved over the preceding forty years, and reduced it to little more than forty per cent of its size at its peak.

The Thatcher counter-revolution was comprehensive in its sweep and its accomplishments. The trade union movement was its first and main target throughout. There was no road to the sort of capitalist regime Thatcher wanted – now known as 'neo-liberalism' – without the reduction of union power to a shadow of its former status, in the workplace, the community and the political process.

The methods used were brazen and, it seemed, politically risky. The first was the abandonment of the commitment to full employment. Allied to a severe squeeze on the economy, applied at a time of deep cyclical recession, this saw the dole queues reach over three million in the early 1980s. Most of the job losses were in the highly unionised manufacturing sector, which contracted by more than fifteen per cent in a matter of three years. This tore the guts out of existing union organisation, and sapped the willingness to fight of those lucky enough to remain in employment. For the first time since the 1930s, the fear of the dole became a major element in

industrial life. The T&G's membership started to decline rapidly –
on Merseyside, long a stronghold of the union, in just a two-year
period it was cut in half, to 50,000.

The second line of attack was changes in the law to hobble
normal trade union operation. Learning from the mistakes of the
Heath government, these changes were introduced piecemeal over
what was ultimately almost the entire period of the Thatcher-Major
governments, and were invariably dressed up as enhancing the
'democratic rights' of trade union members themselves. Thatcher
also avoided proposals which could have led to the imprisonment of
individual trade unionists, thereby reducing the possibility of a
repeat of the 'Pentonville Five' scenario that had so damaged the
earlier Tory government. Instead, trade unions as collective bodies
found their traditional legal protections stripped away.

Mass picketing was outlawed, as was the closed shop. Secret
postal ballots, very slow to conduct, became mandatory before
industrial action could be lawfully undertaken. Any form of solidarity

*Fighting for jobs: women workers occupy the Phillips Rubber
factory in Manchester 1984*

or supportive action was declared illegal. Strike-breakers could no longer be disciplined by the union. A crude attempt to break the unions' support for the Labour Party by mandating ballots on maintaining a political fund was also launched, but this became just about the only anti-union measure to misfire, since trade unionists without exception voted to retain the funds.

Initially, the TUC pledged to defy the laws and organised 'days of action' against them, but the unity of the movement crumbled with the growth of a newly assertive right wing, more hostile to the left in the unions than to the government. The election of first Terry Duffy and then Bill Jordan as leaders of the engineering union, both hard right-wingers, brought to an end the centrally important alliance of the country's two biggest unions that had been formed by Jack Jones and Hugh Scanlon. Undoubtedly, too, the Wilson-Callaghan years had seen the evisceration of the spirit of struggle abroad in the early 1970s. The leaders were not holding back a mass tide of militant sentiment at the grass roots. Such a mood no longer existed in most quarters. Where it did, sections of the movement were left to fight and be defeated one at a time – during Thatcher's first term, steel workers, car workers (with the sacking of Longbridge convenor Derek Robinson) and train drivers were all seen off by the government.

It should not be forgotten that these legal moves were bitterly opposed by the Labour front bench at the time. Gordon Brown, then a T&G sponsored MP, roundly condemned them. He was particularly incensed that 'as a result of these laws, the courts are already eroding the right to picket and to take sympathetic action in support of fellow workers'. The new law was in breach of the International Labour Convention, he added, and had been modelled on the proposals of Professor Hayek, who had said that 'the Conservative government's greatest achievement was to create three million unemployed'. Brown also denounced the legislation on the grounds that it meant that 'the government would be able to curtail the basic right of workers to strike', and would enable employers 'to take unions to court if they don't follow Tory dictated rules for pre-strike ballots'. Sure enough, in December 1984 the *Record* was reporting that the union had been fined £200,000 for backing its striking members at Austin Rover.[1]

One other factor, often neglected, played its part in the diminution of solidarity and militancy – the Tory policy of the sale of council houses, which turned millions of trade unionists from being tenants into mortgage-holders. Ford Dagenham shop steward Dora Challingworth summed up the difference this made succinctly: 'when they were allowed to buy their own houses from Margaret Thatcher's era ... obviously they're not going to come out on strike because they're buying their house now – they're not renting it. They couldn't go up the social and get their rent paid'.[2]

All these elements combined to suck much of the air out of the trade union movement. As Tony Benn puts it: 'that was Mrs Thatcher's skill. She made trade unionism so powerless in law that people said, "why join?" In the process she achieved her over-riding objective, which was restoring the more-or-less untrammelled right of the ruling class to rule as it pleased'.[3]

The 1984-5 miners strike

The 1984-85 miners strike against pit closures became the emblematic dispute of the decade and, indeed, of a generation. Its defeat was the most significant setback for the trade union movement since the 1926 General Strike. It marked the finality of Mrs Thatcher's ascendancy over the labour movement, and the passing of the era in which trade unions were a central force in British politics. During the dispute no union in the country did more to support the National Union of Mineworkers than the T&G. When the miners first came out on strike the T&G pledged unqualified support in the May 1984 *Record*. 'We won't let them starve' was the headline, based on a speech by Moss Evans.

Open cast miners in the T&G voted to stop movement of coal

from their pits, dockers voted for an all-out strike if any member was suspended for blocking coal imports, power and haulage workers refused to handle the movement of coal, Scottish fish porters handed over the day's catch to feed miners' families, and the agricultural group gave the use of its offices to the miners organising pickets. The union also made considerable financial assistance available to the NUM – an increasingly complex operation as the law was used to sequester the miners' funds.

The miners' union president Arthur Scargill responded:

The support of the T&G has been a magnificent boost to the NUM campaign to save our pits, our jobs, and our communities. By halting the movement of coal, by honouring picket lines, transport workers show their determination to save not only coal but British industry as a whole from the wanton butchers of Tory government policies.

Frances O'Grady recalls that her brother was a striking miner in an area where the majority were still working, and that it was important for the minority who were on strike to know that the Transport and General Workers Union were 'not just giving warm words but were giving very practical funding'. The T&G 'was a beacon' at that time, in her words, to an increasingly beleaguered labour movement.[4]

Indeed, the T&G leadership took it as the union's responsibility to do all it could to maintain the strength and morale of the movement and the left within it. It was for this reason that it acted slowly to reduce the union's infrastructure and expenditures in line with its falling membership, a delay which led to a most serious financial crisis in the early 1990s.

However, the broader shift of opinion within the trade unions generally could not but impact on the T&G. The difficulties this caused within the union became more acute when, after the 1983 electoral debacle for Labour, Neil Kinnock, as the Party's new leader, began to shift policy to the right. The new party positions –

most notably on nuclear disarmament – brought it into conflict with the T&G, or at least the majority of its leadership.

This circumstance coincided with emerging difficulties within the union itself. Moss Evans, plagued by ill health, decided to retire early. The main contenders to succeed him were Ron Todd, the union's national organiser, who was supported by the powerful Broad Left, and the Welsh Regional Secretary George Wright. The result of the vote showed Todd the clear victor, but it was marred by allegations of ballot-rigging in some union branches – which is where voting was conducted, in accordance with T&G rules and tradition. These allegations were amplified and doubtless exaggerated in the press since the revelations did no harm at all to the Tory clamour for reform of trade union's internal democratic procedures. Todd declined to take office under a cloud, and insisted on a re-ballot. He won this, too, by a convincing margin, testimony to the continuing power of the Broad Left in the T&G. However, elements within the union, including some of the powerful regional secretaries, never really accepted the legitimacy of Todd's election, and sought to oppose him, mainly through the medium of members of the Executive. When this opposition was able to fuse with groups that differed from the leadership over Labour policy, as the right wing in the party regained momentum, the stage was set for something like civil war within the T&G. And all this was happening at a time when the union was facing the most severe assault from outside, and was confronting the need to take tough decisions flowing from the rapidly declining membership figures. Executive elections became very closely fought, dividing along political lines – and at one stage the work of the GEC was brought to a halt by an unprecedented walk-out by the anti-Todd elements (a minority, but a large one). This was, of course, meat and drink to those in the establishment who wished to see the T&G, the central pillar of progressive trade unionism, brought low. It was no surprise when it was learned years later that the union's chairman at the time, London docker Brian Nicholson, had been a collaborator with the state security services.[5]

It is therefore fair to say that no T&G General Secretary had a more difficult period in office than Ron Todd, an extremely popular man who was the first T&G leader to hail from the motor industry, his working background being in Ford's huge Dagenham plant. He had subsequently run Region One, the T&G's largest, covering London and the south-east, before becoming National Organiser. While much of his time in office was spent endeavouring to persuade the Executive to face up to the financial consequences of membership decline, coping with scandal (an ambitious but ultimately unsuccessful attempt was made to rig the first executive election to be held under a legally enforced postal ballot), and wrestling with political divisions, he managed to maintain an enviable reputation for personal and political integrity.

Much of this he invested in maintaining the T&G's long commitment to nuclear disarmament, a tradition under pressure from the Labour Party leadership from the late 1980s onwards. Less controversially, but with equal passion, he campaigned against apartheid South Africa and the Thatcher government's complicity in the maintenance of the racist regime there. He also secured a place in the hearts of members of the trade union movement with his famous retort to Eric Hammond, leader of the ultra-right and strike-breaking electricians' union, in the course of a debate on the miners' strike at the 1985 Labour Party conference. After Hammond had offensively compared the miners to 'lions led by donkeys', Todd – a genuine animal-lover – told delegates to riotous applause that he would 'rather have a donkey than a jackal'. A man with more 'hinterland' than most union general secretaries, Todd was also an avid collector of fossils and Victorian sheet music.

None of these qualities, of course, dispatched the difficulties the T&G was confronting by the end of the 1980s, including an intransigently hostile political environment, contracting membership and bitter divisions over strategy and perspective. Gradually,

Motor industry leaders: Jack Adams (left), later deputy general secretary and Tony Woodley, later general secretary

Ron Todd unveils a labour movement commemoration

however, the elements of crisis started to abate and, if the decline of the union was by no means reversed, it was at least slowed to manageable proportions. The Executive, pushed by Todd and his deputy Bill Morris, finally bit the bullet and agreed to cut the union's cloth according to circumstances, a painful process involving redundancies and office closures around the country. Leading executive members from both right and left, most notably highly influential London taxi driver Peter Hagger, having peered over the brink for long enough, started to establish some form of consensus about taking the union forward. And the Tory assault on trade unionism eventually started to run out of steam with Mrs Thatcher's eviction from office in 1990, although this was in large measure because it had accomplished all that the establishment had dared hope for in 1979 and more besides.

More mergers

A bright spot for the union in the otherwise dismal decade was three significant mergers with other unions – the last major amalgamations of the T&G's history, as it turned out. The first was with the National Union of Agricultural and Allied Workers.

The NUAAW still had around 70,000 members in 1982, but its finances were under severe pressure from contracting agricultural employment, which was then falling at a rate of over 10,000 per year. This obviously limited possibilities for the union to retrieve its position. The T&G was the obvious choice for a merger partner, since it was the only other union with an agricultural membership (albeit a very much smaller one). While merger had been rejected previously by the agricultural workers, this time members voted by six to one, on a turnout of over 50 per cent, to enter into the T&G, bringing with them a history that stretched back to the Tolpuddle Martyrs. Jack Boddy, then the NUAAW's general secretary, welcomed the ballot result:

We will now have the stability from which we can redouble our efforts to attack the problems which face agricultural and allied workers – low pay, poor and unsafe working conditions and the catastrophic decline in rural amenities ... We still have much unfinished business to get on with. We are happy to do so in common with our urban trade union brothers and sisters.[6]

The merger was also endorsed by *The Countryman*, which editorialised:

Farmers tell us what an efficient industry agriculture is, but it is hard to think of any other in which men handling tens of thousands of pounds' worth of complex equipment and exercising all the traditional skills of livestock care would be paid so little. Ernest Bevin, who created the TGWU, would surely have had a warm welcome for the farm workers ... As a union leader his aim was to get workers in one industry to help those in another. If that now happens in agriculture we shall see a swift advance in that £70.40 a week. Few dairy farmers could withstand blacking by drivers of milk-tankers, nor barley barons' interruption to their supplies of fertilisers and insecticides.[7]

The second major merger was with the Dyers and Bleachers Union, based in Bradford and with a considerable membership across Lancashire and Yorkshire. The T&G had a pre-existing membership in the textile industry, the product of many amalgamations down the years with the often very localised and sectoral union organisations in that industry, but this latest merger provided the basis at last for a national trade group for textile workers. Alas, in both cases – agriculture and textiles – the T&G was unable to shelter its newest groups from the ravages of sustained employment decline, and at the time of the merger with Amicus these were two of the union's smallest trade groups. However, falling numbers also affected longer established trade groups, such as Docks and

Waterways. This last group was reinforced by the transfer of the Stevedores Union into the T&G in the same year as the agricultural and textile unions, which finally established the complete unity of docks trade unionism (outside of a few north-eastern ports where the GMB retained a membership). But this was now an industry only a shadow of its former numerical strength.

The merger that got away – again – during the Tory years was with the GMB. The two unions this time got as far as agreeing in principle to amalgamate, and established a number of working groups to examine practicalities. However, the entrenched power of the GMB's regional secretaries proved an insuperable stumbling block, since no plausible structure for a merged union could retain such a devolution of control and authority. The GMB withdrew from the project – not for the last time, as it turned out. Nor did a plan to merge with the National Union of Mineworkers after the 1984-85 strike prosper, falling apart over the issue of what position Arthur Scargill should be given within the T&G.

Women in the union

Equality was another area in which progress was made during the Tory years. Women were now almost half the workforce, and their representation by and within the T&G had long since passed the point of being an 'add-on' to an essentially male institution. The recruitment and organisation of women workers was central to any prospect of the T&G re-establishing its central place in the labour force.

Much of this work was led by Margaret Prosser, the union's national secretary for women, and a more central figure in the union than previous holders of the office. Her initial efforts to promote the recruitment of women ran, if not into a brick wall, then at least into the stiff resistance of inertia and apathy. Moss Evans 'wasn't interested and didn't really like the idea', she recalls, 'unlike Ron Todd, who had a general gut feeling about fairness extending

Link-Up: Targeting temporary and part-time workers

to all sorts of people, including women'. 'Ron didn't get it that you therefore had to do things to make that fairness come about but nevertheless he felt better about it ... than Moss Evans did'.[8]

In 1987 the union launched a 'Link-Up' campaign, on behalf of the country's six million temporary and part-time workers, the majority of whom were women. Ron Todd said the T&G would be campaigning for temporary and part-time workers to have the same rights as permanent and full-time ones – the same pay and conditions, the same protection against unfair dismissal, and the same training and health and safety representation. 'That really struck a chord with women', Prosser says. 'And the trade union movement was beginning to see that if for no other reason than to keep their membership up, women were the future.'

The campaign was supported by Labour Party leader Neil Kinnock, who said that the government's attack on the rights and security of temporary and part-time workers was 'part of their purpose of creating a disposable, submissive, subordinate labour force'.[9]

Margaret Prosser: a leader in the fight for equal pay

However, problems remained. Brenda Sanders, later the T&G's first and last woman Chair, recalls the difficulties in the way of women who wanted to become active in the union: 'the barriers are the same as they've always been ... children, family, jobs. If you've got a family and a job, it's hard to find that extra time on a Saturday morning or a Sunday or an evening in the week to attend branch meetings and all that'. But, she added – this in an interview in 2008 – 'more men are coming round to the idea of women's involvement now'. Slow progress indeed![10]

The 1989 dock strike

One of the consequences of the miners' defeat was a general retreat of the left in the trade unions, and the growth of 'social partnership' as an alternative strategy – something which closely parallels developments after 1926, with the Mond-Turner talks. Although supported by the TUC and a number of the larger trade unions, this attempt to proceed on the basis of collaboration with employers was doomed, because of the weakness of the trade union position and the undimmed hostility of the government – if for no other reason.

Both the hostility and the weakness were on display in 1989 when the Thatcher government decided to abolish the National Dock Labour Scheme and remove state regulation from employment in the docks industry. The T&G's national docks committee had long declared that it would meet any such government proposal with strike action. However, when the moment arrived it was found that such a response would be unlawful, since it would constitute strike action not against the employer but against the government and parliament. Ron Todd had to use all his influence to prevail on the dockers to hold back from a course of action which, if pursued, would have left the union open to unlimited fines, sequestration and bankruptcy. Instead, the union demanded a national agreement from the National Association of Port Employers to replace the abolished scheme, and when the latter, unsurprisingly, rejected this proposal, since they stood to benefit most from the deregulation of labour in the ports, it was able to call a lawful strike. This availed the union little, however. When the strike started it transpired that in many of the smaller ports covered by the scheme, most registered dockworkers were prepared to take redundancy; and since dockers in the increasingly important ports outside the scheme continued to work normally, the strike had little of the impact it would have had a generation earlier. The Port of London Authority – now centred around Tilbury, the upstream docks in London itself having long since closed – took things a stage further by derecognising the union and dismissing all its shop stewards. The latter eventually secured handsome compensation for unfair dismissal, but the T&G was now excluded from the port where it had first emerged into life, and the strike was called off, defeated. This was perhaps the nadir in the union's industrial fortunes.

Jack Jones believes the union could have responded differently to the government's challenge in the docks:

> The spirit was hounded out of us by Thatcherism, quite deliberately so. And we reacted in a rather constitutional way … when the National Dock Labour Scheme was abolished it should have been challenged straightway by strike action, because that was something of strategic value that we had. Now we've lost the docks membership. We've lost the one area where we could organise solidarity action.

On it being put to him that the law made this course of action difficult, Jones responds with a firm 'the law has always been against us'.[11]

Bill Morris as leader

While the position of T&G general secretary had by the early 1990s lost some of the lustre associated with it in the times of Bevin, Cousins and Jones – no-one would have any longer pretended that

Ron Todd and Bill Morris

the incumbent was 'the most powerful man in the country' – it remained one of the most significant in trade unionism, and to some extent emblematic of the outlook and changes in the working class.

It was therefore rightly regarded as a landmark development when Ron Todd was succeeded at the head of the T&G by his deputy Bill Morris. Morris was the first black general secretary of a British trade union, and his election was both an immense personal achievement and a source of pride for the membership of the union as a whole.

Originally from Jamaica, the young Morris had arrived in Britain in the early 1950s. He worked in the engineering industry in Birmingham in the 1950s and 1960s, at a time when such employment would have been no bed of roses for a young black worker. During Jack Jones's period of leadership Morris became the first black member to be elected to the union's General Executive Council and was then appointed an officer in the midlands region.

He subsequently transferred to London as the national secretary for the bus industry, and from there was promoted to deputy general secretary, after a candidate better placed with the dominant Broad Left decided to stand aside. While the number two has generally been favourite to step up to the top job in the T&G, Morris's election to succeed Todd (to whom he had been a loyal and supportive deputy) was not uncontested. He had to see off a strong challenge from George Wright, the long-standing regional secretary in Wales, who had the support of the Labour Party leadership and the anti-Todd elements throughout the union. No doubt race played a part in mobilising some of the opposition to Morris, but any opposition was clearly extremely unlikely to overcome the advantages he secured from being number two in the union already, from having the support of the powerful Broad Left machine around the country, and from his own personal qualities.

George Foulkes, then a shop steward at Dagenham, recalls the impact of the election:

> When Bill Morris became general secretary there was this euphoria in the black community and we were all saying we never thought it was possible for a black man to be elected into that position ... The T&G was the most progressive left-of-centre union and it's interesting that at one point we had a black General Secretary and a woman as deputy.

Foulkes added, however, that the union 'never embedded that in the culture, into the psyche, that that was how an organisation should be, it should always reflect the diversity of its members'.[12]

Morris's record on equalities was one of the more impressive aspects of his leadership. The rules were changed to enhance the number of women and black members on the executive, making the T&G the only major union to ensure that these hitherto disadvantaged groups were represented on the highest union bodies in a proportion actually in excess of their share of the membership as a whole. And the union's equalities sector was entrenched with a status equivalent to that of its industrial sectors, with committees at all levels to encourage the development of activists who might otherwise have been overlooked in the prevailing culture. As Foulkes indicates, when Jack Adams retired as deputy general secretary in 1998, Margaret Prosser was elected to succeed him, sending the T&G into the new millennium with a black man and a woman as its top team.

The personal commitment of Bill Morris on these issues never wavered. Indeed, he led a high-profile campaign against the Labour government's disgraceful treatment of asylum seekers in the last years of his own leadership of the union, succeeding in getting the vouchers system for refugees scrapped.

Morris also worked to stabilise the union after its period of internal strife and financial difficulties, modernising its management and working to build a consensus on tackling the difficulties of an unfavourable industrial and political climate. This was at a time when membership was falling once more, as the economy re-entered

One Union: Bill Morris works for unity

recession in the early 1990s. Meanwhile the internal problems in the union were exacerbated by an emerging split within the Broad Left, between a faction mainly based in the union's London/South-Eastern and Scottish regions, and one mainly located in the North-West. No great difference of principle was involved but the rift, eventually healed, was a symptom of the T&G's decline as much as anything. It further complicated efforts on the union Executive to chart a united way forward, and led to a serious build-up of pressure on Bill Morris's leadership.

A further factor – the election of Tony Blair as leader of the Labour Party in 1994 – was to combine with these other difficulties to lead to an epic clash over the union's future in 1995. Blair immediately embarked on a revision of Labour's values and principles, removing its constitutional commitment to socialism and making clear his desire to end trade union affiliation to the party – and indeed his distaste for the way unions conducted their business altogether. Blair's drive to 'modernise' the party inevitably led him

*Four general secretaries: (from left) Jack Jones, Bill Morris,
Ron Todd and Moss Evans*

to seek to secure sympathetic leaders in the larger unions, and his burgeoning popularity at that time made it appear that there were no worlds New Labour could not conquer.

This external element fused with the internal problems when Bill Morris had to submit himself for re-election as general secretary. He was the first T&G leader to have to seek a second term in office, as a consequence of the general regulation of unions' internal business introduced by the Tories. All his predecessors had been elected by the membership once, with a right to serve until retirement. Morris would have been obliged by the new laws to seek a fresh mandate in 1996, but he decided to bring forward the ballot by a year, in order to deal with the destabilising pressures building up in the union. His opponent was Jack Dromey, famous from the Grunwick strike nearly twenty years earlier, and in 1995 the union's energetic and well regarded national secretary for public services, the biggest trade group by then. Morris was supported by most of the left and the majority of regional secretaries, while Dromey was backed by a coalition which ranged from the left-wing in the north-west region (incensed by action taken by Morris over alleged maladministration and malfeasance within the region) through to the Blair leadership of the Labour Party. The contest rapidly became confrontational; there was bitterness about an attempt to use Tory laws to unseat Britain's first black trade union leader, and this was compounded by a sense that the Labour leadership was interfering in the affairs of the T&G. The actual strengths and weaknesses of Morris's record in office were overlooked in what became a totemic battle over the union's future.

In the event, Morris secured re-election by 159,000 votes to 100,000 for Dromey, the 33 per cent turnout being exceptionally high for an election conducted by postal ballot – testimony to the unusual interest aroused. Speaking at his victory celebration, Morris declared 'we have stopped a juggernaut in its tracks' – referring to Blair's New Labour. Alas, that proved to be an optimistic reading of the outcome, but the poll certainly showed the limit of Blair's reach in the unions, and it would be some time before he would attempt such brazen interference again.

Two disputes

The 1990s were uncertain years for what was basically a defeated trade union movement. An atmosphere of retreat and retrenchment set in, as leaders felt they could do little beyond hope for a change in the political weather. Morale and rank-and-file activism tended to decline in the T&G and, while the union retained its progressive political principles, these were no longer advocated with the urgency of earlier years.

Instead, a new emphasis was placed on partnership with employers and services to members. In the latter respect, a milestone was passed in 1994 when the T&G became the first major trade union to provide round-the-clock free legal advice to its members and their families – an estimated three million people in all. 'This unique service is the best possible evidence of our determination to move as much of our resources as possible into giving T&G members the best', said Bill Morris as he launched the legal helpline in the *Record*. The union also put exceptional campaigning energy into fighting low pay, arguing both for a statutory national minimum wage to be introduced by Labour whenever it returned to office, and for a £4 an hour minimum in industrial negotiations.

Despite his efforts to build better relations with employers, the Morris years at the T&G will be better remembered for two very different industrial disputes. The first, a particularly painful one for the union, was on the Liverpool docks – one of the few former 'scheme ports' where the union had retained a strong organised presence after the 1989 strike. The dispute arose because of job losses at a small stevedoring company at the port – a situation which would, under the National Dock Labour Scheme, have resulted in the workers' re-employment by the Mersey Docks and Harbour Company. As it was, the redundant men mounted a picket, which

Tackling Low Pay: The T&G's £4 Now hotline

the much larger number of dockers employed directly by MDHC (many of them relatives of the stevedores) refused to cross. The employer then took the opportunity to dismiss them, since their refusal to cross the picket line constituted unlawful industrial action on several counts. A bitter row erupted as to whether union officials had properly advised the strikers as to what the likely consequence of such action would have been, and whether an offer by MDHC which could have averted the strike had been passed on. These questions remain without agreed answer to this day.

At any event, the T&G leadership made every effort to support the locked out dockers within the tightly drawn framework of the law. They were given considerable material support, but no industrial solidarity or other action that, in Morris's view, could have exposed the union to the threat of considerable losses as a result of legal proceedings. The dockers themselves organised massive support from port workers around the world, but increasingly regarded their own union as at best impotent in the face of the law, and at worst conniving with the employers to force them to accept the end of the dispute on unsatisfactory terms. The whole issue boiled over into a vitriolic row at the 1997 Biennial Delegate Conference. But such episodes did not practically advance the Liverpool dockers' cause and, once the newly elected Labour government had made it clear that it was not going to lift a finger to resolve the matter, the dispute was abandoned in 1998. That was not, however, the end of the issue, and some of the dockers, feeling bitterly betrayed, pursued legal action against the union itself. This was only finally resolved in 2007. The whole dispute highlighted in the most stark terms the difficulties faced by British trade unions – almost uniquely in the western world – in trying to conduct their ordinary business within the law.

The second dispute was a happier experience for the union. This saw it take on and defeat one of Britain's best known and biggest companies, British Airways, on behalf of its cabin crew membership. The company, seeking major cuts in its operations, decided to take an axe to the pay and conditions of stewards and stewardesses. This would have been bad enough, but, still worse, BA made it clear that its real aim was to break the union. To this end it used a small breakaway organisation, Cabin Crew 89, as a stalking horse to accept the company's proposals, and ran a crude campaign of intimidation against their employees, warning them that they could not just be sacked but even imprisoned for taking strike action! An attempt to whip up a media campaign against the kind of employees that more enlightened airlines actually used as a marketing tool backfired badly. Three days of industrial action were taken, resulting in disastrous financial losses to the company and still greater damage to its image and reputation. The dispute was notable for the number of cabin crew who, having been threatened by their managers, decided to phone in sick on the strike days (something the company was not able to challenge or question), leading to the dispute being remembered as the 'sicknote strike'. The company came to an agreement with the union soon after, representing a rare high-profile industrial victory for the T&G in the 1990s, and a personal success both for Bill Morris and for the national secretary for the industry, George Ryde, who had led from the front. The outcome saw off attempts to derecognise the union and helped entrench the T&G in a growing industry. The fact that most of the media was sympathetic to the strikers and critical of BA's ham-fisted bullying was an indicator of the changing industrial environment as the Thatcher years receded into the past.

The New Labour era

'Now, at last, we can look forward to a future of dialogue, not head-banging', said Bill Morris in May 1997, as the Tories' 18-year run in office came to a spectacular end with Labour's election landslide:

> T&G members will understand what Labour's historic and unprece-
> dented victory on May 1 means. It means a minimum wage and a

long overdue attack on poverty pay. It means an attack on the crime of mass unemployment, particularly among the young. It means signing up to the social chapter, and restoring to employees at GCHQ the right to be members of a trade union.

He concluded: 'What we want is what Labour has promised – a fair deal for working people'.[13]

Certainly, trade unionists could be forgiven for thinking that with Labour back in office the worst was over. And the new government did initially deliver on some of its pledges – a minimum wage was introduced, unions did secure the right to recognition (under a somewhat cumbersome procedure) and John Major's opt-out from the EU social chapter was abandoned. Unemployment was also kept low, although this was masked by very large numbers of the long-term jobless claiming disability benefits.

However, the bulk of the anti-union laws remained on the statute book. Indeed, Tony Blair actually boasted that Britain had the toughest union regulations in Europe. And the new government was fully signed up to the new neo-liberal consensus, promoting privatisation, deregulation (of everything except trade unionism) and free markets. Both Blair and Chancellor Gordon Brown were enthusiastically pro-big business and the Prime Minister was also a starstruck admirer of the very wealthy. Brown was more interested in making gestures towards trade union sensibilities – and one such gesture was the appointment of Bill Morris as a director of the Bank of England.

As it turned out, neither membership nor morale received a significant boost from the change in the political scene, and the prevailing sense of drift was not dissipated. Morris's tough management skills had hauled the T&G back from the brink of terminal crisis, but there was little by way of a clear perspective for the future. Indeed, among all the larger unions at the time, only the AEEU displayed a real sense of purpose – and the purpose of its leader, Sir Ken Jackson, was to offer whatever was required to any employer to secure recognition for his union, even if it was at the expense of another TUC affiliate. The T&G went nowhere near as far as the AEEU in its pursuit of 'business trade unionism', nor in its support for anything and everything the government did or said. But echoes of the same attitudes were to be found, despite the union's democratic and progressive culture and traditions. This was reflected in the ideas of 'social partnership', which became a sort of dogma at the TUC for a time. Morris, while remaining willing to support members in struggle (unlike the AEEU of the time), was attracted to this thinking.

This would not have commended itself to its predecessors. Jack Jones's view was typically abrupt: 'It's terrible. It's an idea that should never have got off the ground. It's an alternative to being militant. Of course, employers were always mouthing it. Had we had stronger leadership here, building up more militancy, we could have been more effective in the field.'[14] And John Cousins, son of Jones's predecessor, warns: 'the concept that we're both on the same side is nonsense – we're not on the same side at all. Never have been, never can be. You can collaborate with each other for mutual benefit but to say that our objectives are the same, they're not.'

Certainly, the trade union movement had little to show for this strategy by the turn of the century. The government was utterly unwilling to engage in anything that smacked of 1970s-style tripartism or corporatism. Its view was that the two sides of industry should get on with it without government involvement. Yet that philosophy ignored the gross imbalance in power of the two sides: and the tilt towards the employers inherent in the capital-labour relationship was reinforced by the continuation on the statute book of most of the Tory laws that made effective trade unionism so difficult.

This lack of real progress on either the industrial or political front provided the background for the last great shift in the T&G's history – a shift which was to at once renew the union and to bring that history to a conclusion.

Notes

1. *T&G Record*, February 1984.
2. Geoffrey Goodman interview.
3. Geoffrey Goodman interview.
4. Geoffrey Goodman interview.
5. www.guardian.co.uk/uk/2001/jan/01/politics.freedomofinformation.
6. Wynn, p126.
7. *The Countryman*, Summer 1982, pp20-21.
8. Geoffrey Goodman interview.
9. Prosser in Goodman interview; Kinnock in *T&G Record*, August 1987.
10. Jack Amos interview.
11. Murray, p35.
12. Geoffrey Goodman interview.
13. *T&G Record*, May 1997.
14. Murray, pp37-38.
15. Geoffrey Goodman interview.

8. Into Unite 2003-2007

The road to the creation of Unite had two different starting points. One of these was the election of Derek Simpson, against all predictions, as general secretary of the engineering union, then midway through its own merger with MSF to form Amicus.

This at a stroke brought to an end the long domination of the AEU (and later the AEEU, as it became following a previous amalgamation with the electricians union) by the right wing. This had reached its nadir under the leadership of the defeated Sir Ken Jackson. The division between the T&G and the engineering union, which had begun after the replacement of Hugh Scanlon by Terry Duffy back in 1977, had for a long time been an important factor in preventing a united trade union response to the immense challenges of Thatcherism and its aftermath. Under Jackson the AEEU appeared to take delight in provoking other trade unions, while at the same time marketing itself to employers with abandon. The AEEU became the main (although not the only) advocate of taking 'partnership' to the point of single-union no-strike deals, in which the membership had little or no say. Under those circumstances, the idea of a strong relationship between the newly amalgamated Amicus and the T&G would have been incredible – let alone a merger. Yet Simpson's leadership opened up the possibility from the outset, if only by taking the union back into the mainstream of the movement, of repairing relations with other TUC affiliates and abandoning the worst of Jackson's industrial relations practices.

Saving Rover

The other point of departure in the pathway towards the creation of the new union is to be found in the battle to save the huge Rover Longbridge car factory, which took place a couple of years before the revolution in the AEEU. There the T&G fought one of the few union struggles of the last generation to achieve some measure of success, and one of the few at any time to have reversed a planned plant closure – always the hardest battles for a union to win. It was the successful conduct of the Longbridge campaign that turned Tony Woodley, at the time the T&G's national secretary for the motor industry, into a popular candidate for the T&G's leadership. Other possible successors to Bill Morris would almost certainly not have pursued the possibility of creating a new union as vigorously.

The Rover plant on the edge of Birmingham had passed into the ownership of the German company BMW, which abruptly decided to off-load it in 2000 as a victim of the excess in production capacity in the global capitalist car market. Its preferred buyer was a private-equity consortium which intended to shut the factory down immediately. This would have cost around 10,000 jobs directly, and many more in the supply chain and in the local economy. The New Labour government was uninterested in intervening, and a mood of fatalism even permeated the higher echelons of the union itself. But Tony Woodley immediately threw himself into the fight to rescue the factory. A 100,000-strong demonstration marched through Birmingham, possibly the largest England's second city has ever seen. Behind the publicity and propaganda, Woodley was working to support a second buyer – a consortium of business people headed by well-known industry executive John Towers. BMW were eventually pressurised into selling to this 'Phoenix' consortium, and Longbridge's future rose from the ashes, with Woodley – rightly – getting much of the credit.

Of course, the Phoenix did not fly for long. As a small player in a market dominated by ever bigger companies, Rover desperately needed an international partner to be able to develop new models, but this not forthcoming. The consortium started running out of money within four years – a situation not helped by the fact that its members were helping themselves most generously (although entirely legally) to the company's cash. While this greediness was bad press for Rover, it was marginal to the ultimate economics of the situation, which culminated in the company's bankruptcy in 2005. After the failure of an ambitious attempt to interest the giant Chinese concern Shanghai Automobile Industries Corporation in buying the factory, Longbridge finally all but closed. However, Woodley's intervention could claim to have brought five years further work, and time for suppliers and the local economy to diversify. Certainly, few trade union campaigns against closures could claim as much. It also propelled Tony Woodley to the front of those looking to succeed Bill Morris: it gave him a media profile, which can count for as much as 'machine' support in a PR-conscious age, especially in a secret postal ballot.

Woodley recognised this advantage himself. Reflecting on the Rover struggle in 2007 he said:

> There's no doubt that events ... make people and there's absolutely no doubt at all [that] whilst I was well-known in the car industry part of the union, it was Rover, the high profile, that actually led to many more people knowing this person. But the most important thing wasn't getting the profile, it was winning for our people at Rover ... I make no apologies for getting too close to members and members' interests.
>
> That was a battle worth winning. It did stop that company falling into the hands of venture capitalists, it did stop 10,000 people literally being sacked on day one, and it gave us those five years to try and find a partner for the company.[1]

Tony Woodley becomes leader

Woodley's election to succeed Bill Morris was far from inevitable, however, even after the Longbridge campaign. For one thing, T&G general secretaries have usually been succeeded by the candidate of their own choosing, and Morris did not choose Woodley. He was unhappy when Woodley was elected as deputy general secretary in 2002, succeeding the retiring Margaret Prosser.

Nevertheless, by 2003 it was clear that trade unionists in general wanted change. In one union after another they were voting for new leaders who were advocating a more adversarial – or at least independent – approach to industrial relations, and a more progressive political stance. Derek Simpson's election had been the most vivid sign of this trend, but it also swept through a number of smaller unions, producing a crop of general secretaries that was

Tony Woodley, ninth and last T&G general secretary

dubbed 'the awkward squad' by sections of the media. The membership of the T&G was far from being immune to this mood, and both Woodley and Jack Dromey, who was a candidate once more, tried to articulate it.

Speaking during the campaign, Woodley made his attitude clear:

> Unions have sometimes got a culture, under partnership principles, where, before they even listen to members' concerns they get the gaffer's 'moderate' view as to why our members should be sacked – there's a mindset that we listen to the employers before we get our members' point of view.[2]

Many members, he noted during the campaign, were now doubtful as to the value to them of trade unionism. What then must non-members feel? He promised an end to 'phoney' social partnership deals, to support members wanting to 'fight back' against employers, and to be more assertive in pushing the union's case with Labour ministers. Evidently, members liked what they heard, electing Woodley as the T&G's ninth and last general secretary in the summer of 2003. Dromey, runner-up in that election, won the ballot to replace Woodley in the deputy's job a few months later.

As already noted, Tony Woodley's roots were in the motor industry, Merseyside and, originally, another union – the National Union of Vehicle Builders – which became part of the T&G in the early 1970s. He had joined the NUVB as a 19 year-old in Vauxhall's Ellesmere Port assembly plant (where his father was works convenor), having previously made his living in the merchant navy. Woodley followed his father as a shop steward and later convenor. T&G chairman Stan Pemberton persuaded him to make an application for a job as a full-time union officer based in Birkenhead, and within a few years he was promoted to national officer in the vehicle building group, working under Jack Adams. He was named its national secretary when Adams left to become deputy to Bill Morris. A left-winger in the progressive T&G tradition, he had spoken on behalf of the union at the two-million-strong anti-war demonstration in February 2003 and, just two weeks before taking up office in October, had called on Tony Blair to resign because of the Iraq war.

A focus on organising

The most important change Woodley introduced during the T&G's last years as a separate union was a new focus on organising – seeking to at long last reverse the union's membership decline, which had thinned its ranks out to around 800,000 by 2003.

This was an area of work where standing still meant moving backwards. The continuing decline of manufacturing industry and the export of jobs to low-wage locations guaranteed a falling membership unless determined corrective action was taken. The days of workers finding their way to trade unions more or less spontaneously were now over. A generation had grown up in workplaces which, while not hostile towards unions, were often barely aware of their existence, and certainly doubtful about their continuing relevance – unsurprisingly, given their greatly weakened state.

Drawing heavily on the experience of US trade unions, particularly the Service Employees Industrial Union, which spent a substantial proportion of their income on organising, Woodley set about reshaping the T&G to become an organising union. Other expenditures were reduced to free funds for hiring a large number of organisers – around eighty by the time of the formation of Unite. These organisers looked like the people they needed to recruit – many were young, female and from ethnic minorities, or even all three.

Over the next three years, and notwithstanding the teething troubles inevitable in such a pioneering venture, the organising initiative, headed by Jack Dromey, scored notable successes, winning recognition and real advances in pay and conditions in hitherto anti-union companies, in civil aviation, food processing and elsewhere. An ambitious effort was also launched to organise the

Organising House of Commons cleaners

contract cleaning workforce – much of it composed of migrant workers – in London's big offices. By these methods, the union was recruiting more than 15,000 additional members annually – over and above the far larger number joining in already organised workplaces. Just as importantly, strong trade union structures were being implanted, with hundreds of new shop stewards and workplace representatives elected in the newly organised companies. 'Winning and Growing' became the mantra, and the organising culture appeared there to stay.

The Gate Gourmet dispute

On the other campaign front to which Woodley was committed – changes in employment law – progress was considerably harder to come by. New Labour in office remained committed to the deregulated labour market, alongside heavily regulated trade unionism. Trade unions affiliated to the Labour Party remained caught between acquiescing in government policy, to the exasperation of many of their active members, or making a fuss and being ignored, demonstrating thereby their political impotence.

The move to the left across all the major unions allowed the 'big four' – Unison, Amicus, the T&G and the GMB – to concert their political activities in a way hardly conceivable before. This gave the unions the votes to defeat the government on a range of social and economic policy issues at Labour's conference. It did not, however, give them the power to make ministers actually pay any attention to what they were saying – even when, as on railway renationalisation, they undoubtedly spoke for the great majority of public opinion.

As ever, it was events in the real world rather than conference debates that made the difference. The campaign for regulation of the practices of 'gangmasters' – suppliers of cheap and often migrant labour to a range of industries, including agriculture – took off after 13 Chinese cockle-pickers were tragically drowned in Morecambe

Bay early in 2004. The T&G led a successful drive for regulation to be placed on the statute book in the wake of the disaster.

Employment law also moved up the political agenda after a major industrial dispute at Heathrow Airport. Gate Gourmet, an airline catering supplier spun off from British Airways, and under pressure from BA to cut costs, dismissed most of their employees at one site (mainly Asian women), after a contrived confrontation aimed at bringing in even cheaper agency labour. The workers were for a time locked in a canteen, while others were sacked by megaphone outside.

The site was near the airport, and other T&G organised workers there – mainly baggage handlers and other ground staff employed by British Airways, some of them related to the Gate Gourmet employees – immediately and spontaneously walked out in protest at this act of brutal management. This closed much of the airport down for 24 hours and cost British Airways a considerable sum. BA bore a large measure of responsibility for the crisis at Gate Gourmet, since it was overwhelmingly the suppliers' main customer and it was BA demands that had led to the pressure for cuts in labour costs. But the action was illegal under the Tory laws that had been carefully left on the statute book by Tony Blair, which prohibit any form of solidarity action between workers in different firms. In accordance with its own conference policy, the union fully complied with the requirements of the law by repudiating the secondary action, since to do otherwise could have put the fabric of the union at risk.

After hard bargaining with the private-equity owners of Gate Gourmet, the union secured reinstatement for many of the more than 700 sacked workers, while most of the rest accepted a pay-off from the company. The more lasting impact of the dispute, however, was its highlighting of the inequity of employment law, which prohibited supportive industrial action in a closely associated company (in defiance of International Labour Organisation conventions), yet allowed the employer to introduce strike-breaking

Fighting Back at Gate Gourmet

Fighting Back on London Buses

agency labour at lower rates of pay with impunity. As a result of this, two months later Tony Woodley was able to win the Labour Party conference, against ministerial opposition, to vote for a change in the law; and more than a hundred MPs, mainly Labour, were persuaded to support a Trade Union Freedom Bill which would somewhat level the legal playing field. Changing New Labour minds proved an uphill struggle, however, and the battle remains to be won at the time of writing. That trade unions should still be fighting for the most elementary rights – many of which are taken for granted in other western countries – twelve years into a Labour government is an extraordinary commentary on the changes that had taken place in the Labour Party. The inability of affiliated trade unions to exert effective influence over the government became a source of increasing frustration. As Jack Jones observed in 2003: 'Something has gone wrong. Not so many people link trade unions with a socialist outlook. Trade unions cannot exist without political action.' Developing effective political action remained a challenge.[3]

Merging with Amicus

The election of Tony Woodley as general secretary, the turn to organising and the more robust political approach certainly helped to rebuild morale within the T&G. However, the chronic underlying difficulties arising from twenty-five years of more or less uninterrupted decline remained. Indeed, in some respects they had worsened. Globalisation was producing renewed pressure on membership levels, particularly in manufacturing, as employers moved work abroad – to Eastern Europe or to Asia. Labour-intensive manufacturing was leaving Britain for ever. The great factories that had long nurtured the T&G's culture were going the way of the docks, at least as major concentrations of labour. In aggregate membership terms, therefore, the organising initiatives still left the union running up a downward-moving escalator.

Inter-union competition and rivalry remained a wasteful diversion. The T&G had by 2003 become only the third biggest union in the country – after Unison, dominant in much of the public sector, and the newly-created Amicus. The latter had itself become something of a general union, with a membership stretching from the traditional AEU base in engineering to health, finance, construction and beyond. Following the incorporation of the print union GPMU and the financial services union Unifi, it spread wider still. The GMB remained on the scene too, of course, slightly smaller than the T&G. The question as to whether – in a rapidly changing labour market with manifold pressures on finances and organising capacity – there was enough room for three general unions was inevitably on the agenda. The workforce was now divided between those (the great majority in the private sector) working in non-union workplaces and those employed in industries where two, three or more unions organised and often competed. The possibility was remote that any trade union – other than those focused on special and stable sections of the economy – could on their own muster sufficient resources and impetus to overcome their problems. For the T&G, as for many others, the choice was change or a lingering decline towards the margins of industrial and political influence – 'the Beazer Homes League' of trade unionism in the words of Woodley, a football fanatic.

From these considerations what became Unite was born. Woodley and Derek Simpson had a strong personal relationship that helped revive, in a very different context, the spirit of the Jones-Scanlon partnership. Their perspectives meshed on many of the challenges facing their unions. Simpson additionally laid great emphasis on the need for a global approach to trade unionism, reflecting the globalisation of capital, while Woodley remained an evangelist for organising.

Nevertheless, when Woodley proposed merging with Amicus to form a new union 'fit to meet the challenges of the twenty-first century' there was considerable anxiety within the T&G. This was unsurprising. While the case for forming the new union was very strong in terms of its industrial logic and the optimal use of resources, trade unions are not companies, where the 'business case' is all. They are living, democratic organisations of working people with their own traditions, embedded in workplaces, communities and, indeed, ways of life. Unlike Amicus, itself the product of a roller-coaster ride of mergers over the preceding fifteen years or so, the T&G had been in uninterrupted independent existence since 1922. Over a hundred unions had merged *into* the T&G but none had merged *with* it on an equal basis. Its activists were proud of its political traditions, of its lay democracy, and of structures which had stood the test of time, with only minor modifications, since the days of Bevin. While no-one could gainsay the changes in Amicus following the election of Simpson, there were inevitable doubts as to how deep-rooted these developments were. What had happened to the old right-wing machine, once so powerful? Would the T&G's advances in terms of structures for women and ethnic minority members be preserved? Could a new union be as democratic as the T&G? And so on.

Initially, the plan was for the new union to be a tripartite venture, with the GMB as the third leg. This was not to be. Karl Marx famously observed that history repeats itself first as tragedy, then as farce. His imagination would have been defeated by the efforts of the T&G and the GMB to form a single general union throughout the twentieth century and into the twenty-first. Familiar problems over the structure of the new union emerged once more in the preliminary discussions, after which the GMB conference voted to end further involvement in the project in 2006, determining instead to remain a free-standing union.

While regrettable – particularly from the perspective of the T&G, which had a considerable overlap of membership with the GMB in many industries – this decision at least allowed the now two-way negotiations to proceed more rapidly. A broad democratic consultation was held throughout the T&G on what the new union should look like and which elements of the T&G's own culture, structure and procedures needed to be carried forward. The negotiations were led by Woodley, with a big part being played by the Chair of the Executive, Jimmy Kelly – the first member from Ireland to hold that high office in the union's history. He was followed in that position by Brenda Sanders, a Merseyside factory worker, who had the distinction of being both the T&G's last Chair and also the first woman to hold the position. She ensured that the union saved itself at the last from the ignominy of having represented working women for 85 years but never having chosen one to hold its highest lay office. Brenda also played a significant part in the merger discussions, particularly in ensuring that the T&G's approach to equality issues was not diluted.

A draft Instrument of Amalgamation was finally produced in the autumn of 2006 and was then the subject of further consultation within the union. It satisfied members on what the T&G's 2005 BDC had set down as 'red-line issues' – lay democracy, the maintenance of equalities structures and the preservation (indeed enhancement) of the organising drive. The T&G's dual structure of authoritative regions and national industrial organisation with appropriate autonomy was maintained, as was the T&G's preference for branches being rooted in the workplace. It was agreed that Woodley and Simpson would lead the new union together for slightly over three years, with a closely coordinated retirement programme to precede a handing over to a single successor, to be elected by the membership.

After further amendments, the Executive approved the Instrument, and the union recalled its BDC to meet in Birmingham shortly before Christmas 2006, to decide on whether to bring the curtain down on the T&G and raise it on the new union – at that stage unnamed. This was preceded by a final, comprehensive, consultation, explaining the Instrument at meetings in every region and with every national trade group committee. By the time delegates assembled in Birmingham most of the arguments had been thrashed out, although that did not diminish the sense of history infusing the proceedings.

Tony Woodley moved the Executive's resolution at the conference. His address, from which these extracts are taken, is as good a place as any to end the T&G story:

> We have lived through a generation of decline in our movement. We have no intention of letting that become a lifetime of decline. The big prize is not this merger, but the millions of workers out there who need trade unionism.
>
> We take into the new union our rock-solid T&G values of fighting for peace and socialism. Values first taken to the national and international stage by Frank Cousins, elected as our general secretary half a century ago this year. Those values – standing for social justice, international solidarity, nuclear disarmament, against racism and imperialism, for a world where poverty, unemployment and discrimination belong in the history books – are T&G values. But they are not the values of the T&G alone.
>
> They are shared wherever working men and women come together to fight for a better world. They are shared in Amicus, too, of course – today more than at any time for a generation.
>
> Today, we reaffirm our commitment to our past, to the achievements and self-sacrifice of the men and women who built

Voting for merger – the last conference meets in
Birmingham, December 2006

Honouring the past, building the future: (from left) Tony Woodley,
Jack Jones, Jimmy Kelly, Jack Dromey

the T&G as the greatest force for social progress in twentieth-century Britain and Ireland.

And we reaffirm that the way – the ONLY way – to genuinely honour that past is to ensure its vitality into the future by building a union as powerful in this century as the T&G was for much of the last.

If this merger is about one thing, it is this: working-class unity, the historic aim of our movement, founded on the realisation that unity makes us stronger. That every trade unionist has far more in common with his brother or sister in a different union than there are things that divide us. When we stand together our opponents in the workplace and society – bad bosses and callous governments – suddenly start to look much smaller.

So judge this by the standards of Bevin and Cousins, of Ron Todd and Jack Jones – giants who left us this great instrument, the Transport and General Workers Union not to let it wither, not to see history pass it by but as a mandate to be renewed in each generation. Meeting the particular challenges of the day in new forms, unafraid to change but steady in its purpose.

Those delegates left unpersuaded were, in the end, numbered in single figures. Three months later, the T&G membership overwhelmingly endorsed the proposal for a new union, as did their brothers and sisters in Amicus in simultaneous ballots. The new union was launched on 1 May 2007. With that, the Unite story began.

Notes

1. Geoffrey Goodman interview.
2. Murray, p176.
3. Murray, p36.

9. In place of a conclusion

We are a movement, not a monument, Scottish miners' leader Mick McGahey once famously observed. An excess of sentiment is therefore inappropriate when considering the lifespan of a working-class organisation. Trade unions exist to serve their members in great ways and small – perhaps more accurately they are the vehicle for those members serving themselves, they are not there to be hung on a wall and admired. And they are the product of social conditions and industrial structures. When these change, so too must the organisations of working people. This does not happen like clockwork, nor are the rhythms of change predictable.

The T&G was the product of industrial Britain and Ireland of the late nineteenth and early twentieth century – its exploitation, its great concentrations of labour, its impoverished working-class communities. Bevin's genius was to build an organisation which could represent all manner of those employed in that world of work, and which could adapt to the changes of the next fifty or sixty years while remaining true to its purpose. The genius of Cousins and Jones was to unlock the democratic potential in such an organisation and ally it to a broader, socialist, perspective of remaking society, a vision Bevin had embraced in his youth but somewhat lost along the way. Tony Woodley and his colleagues realised that whatever the T&G represented, it could only remain a vital force in society through a transformation greater than it could conceivably hope to accomplish from within itself.

The balance sheet of the union's history will always be disputed. There are many who will contend that such a powerful organisation could and should have achieved more for the working class. They will point to the bureaucratic habits and procedures that are an inevitable accretion of orderly industrial life, and which at times threatened to overwhelm the democratic vitality of the union. Others will highlight the many ways in which the union reflected the more limited, or even negative, trends and habits within the life of the labour movement. Far greater in number and louder in volume are those critics who will damn the T&G as they damn all fighting trade unions, for representing an unconscionable violation of the rules of the free market and an overweening aspiration to tell their betters how society should be ordered.

Whatever view one takes, the influence of the T&G and its traditions will be felt for many years to come – most obviously within Unite, the union which is the direct successor to the Transport and General Workers Union. They will also be felt within the Labour Party and the left, and in the large number of communities in which it was a major institution, and sometimes the most dynamic and powerful one. There is no alchemy in this – the traditions are those of working-class self-organisation, collective involvement and struggle and democratic control. Eventually, the echo of the T&G as an organisation will fade and become inaudible, but those traditions will mutate, develop, cross-fertilise and move on. Unite itself will only be a way station. The T&G spoke for eighty-five years in the authentic tones of the working class of these islands. The next great trade union unity conference will most likely be conducted in many tongues.

103, 106, 115, 117, 140, 141, 144, 167, 173, 186, 198, 209
Equal pay, 39, 87, 102, 146-7, 183
Esso, 132
European Union, 195; *see also* EEC
Evans, Moss, 145, 181, 183, 189
– as General Secretary, 167-9, 174-6

Fascism, fascists, 72-5, 77, 108, 152
Feather, Victor, 150, 157
Foot, Michael, 164
Ford motor company, 102, 143, 144, 145, 169, 174, 177
– sewing machinists strike, 146-7
Forden, Len, 132
Foulkes, George, 187, 188
Franco, General, 72, 157

Gaitskell, Hugh, 123, 124, 127
Gander, Alexander, 62
Gangmasters regulation, 205-6
Gas Workers Union, 22
Gate Gourmet dispute, 206-8
General & Municipal Workers Union, see GMB
General Strike 1926, 49-53, 56, 59, 79, 174
General unionism, 14-16, 21-2, 27, 35, 40; *see also* new unionism
Gill, Ken, 140
GMB (formerly General & Municipal Workers Union), 16, 41, 55, 56, 97, 103, 123, 181, 205, 209, 211
Gosling, Harry, 35, 37, 41, 47, 70
GPMU, 209
Grunwick, 139, 161, 190

Hagger, Peter, 179
Halpin, Kevin, 134
Hammond, Eric, 177
Hancock, Florence, 56
Hawley, Greville, 160
Healey, Denis, 163, 169
Healey, Tom, 116
Heath, Edward, 154, 157, 164, 169, 172
Heathrow Airport, 120, 206
Henderson, Sam, 109
Hirst, Stanley, 37, 39

Hitler, Adolph, 72, 73, 77, 78, 84
Hobbs, Fred, 56
Holmes, Andy, 137
Horner, Arthur, 96, 97
Humber-Rootes strike, 100
Hyndman, H.M., 20

Imperial Typewriters dispute, 161-2
In Place of Strife, 133-4, 154
Incomes policy, wage restraint, 97, 98, 99, 117, 118, 127, 128, 129, 131, 132, 136, 137, 163, 164, 165, 166, 169
Independent Labour Party, 24
Industrial Relations Act 1971, 154-5
Industrial relations laws, employment laws, 23, 24, 25, 37, 53, 63, 84, 163, 172-4, 175, 184, 185, 190, 193, 195, 196, 205, 206, 208; *see also, In Place of Strife*; Industrial Relations Act 1971; Taff Vale Judgement; Osborne judgement
International Brigades, 74, 75, 141
Ireland, 15, 27, 42, 43, 157-8, 159, 211, 214, 215
Irish Transport and General Workers Union, 27, 157

Jackson, Ken, 195, 198
Jenkins, Roy, 157
Jolly George, 30
Jones, Bill, 64, 65, 70, 75, 128, 135
Jones, Jack, 18, 59, 71, 72, 74, 75, 81, 85, 87, 89, 94, 95, 96, 110, 112, 115, 118, 128, 132, 133, 134, 135, 168, 173, 185, 186, 189, 196, 208, 210, 213, 214, 215
– as General Secretary, 141-67
Jordan, Bill, 173

Kelly, Jimmy, 211, 213
Kershaw, Herbert, 70
Kinnock, Neil, 175, 183
Kitson, Alex, 159, 161
Korean War, 98, 110,

Labour Party, 24-5, 30, 31, 70, 72, 73-4, 77, 79, 82, 90-1, 93, 97, 106, 110, 117, 121, 122-5, 129, 135,

136, 137, 156, 173, 175, 176, 177, 183, 187, 189, 208, 216
– Labour government 1924, 48
– Labour government 1929-31, 57-59
– Labour government 1945-51, 93, 97, 98, 114
and Ernest Bevin, 93, 97-8
– Labour government, 1964-70, 127-32, 133-4
and Frank Cousins, 127-32
and *In Place of Strife*, 133-4
– Labour government, 1974-79, 158, 162-5
and social contract, 162-5
and 'winter of discontent', 169-70
– Labour government 1997-, 188, 193, 194-5, 199, 205, 208; *see also* Blair, Tony
– New Labour, 98, 189-90, 193, 194-5, 199, 205, 208, 216; *see also* Blair, Tony
Labour Representation Committee, 25
Lambourn Stables, Berkshire, 68
Lansbury, George, 73-4
Larkin, Jim, 27, 157
Law, Alan, 118
Lawther, Will,
Liaison Committee for the Defence of Trade Unions, 134, 154
Liberal government 1905-15, 25
Liberal Party, 15, 22, 24, 25, 165
Liebknecht, Karl, 49
Lightermen, Lightermen's Union, 40, 103, 160
Link-Up campaign, 182, 183
Liverpool docks strike, 191, 193
Lloyd George, David, 27, 30, 31, 32
London Docks Strike 1889, 17-21
Longbridge, 117, 119, 144, 173, 199-200, 201
Luxemburg, Rosa, 49

MacDonald, Ramsay, 48, 57-9, 165
Macleod, Iain, 118
Macmillan, Harold, 118, 151
Mann, Tom, 17-18, 19, 22, 55
Marx, Karl, 20, 58, 211

Match Girls strike, 15, 16, 19
McCullough, Ellen, 56
Membership levels, 66, 87, 102, 106, 118, 160, 172, 175, 176, 177, 188, 203, 209
Miners, mining industry, 27, 31, 59, 65, 67, 84, 94, 156, 157
– 1984-5 miners strike, 174-5, 177, 184
see also general strike, 1926; National Union of Mineworkers
Morris Motor Company, 67, 110
Morris, Bill, 152, 179, 199, 200, 201, 202
– as General Secretary, 185-196
Morrison, Herbert, 58, 90
Mosley, Oswald, Mosleyites, 72, 73, 74
Motor industry, *see* car industry
MSF, 198
Mussolini, Benito, 72

National Association of Operative Plasterers, 13
National Dock Labour Board, 105, 211
National Dock Labour Corporation, 83
National Dock Labour Scheme, 103, 104, 184, 185, 191
National Front, 151
National government 1929-35, 58, 61, 73
National Industrial Relations Court, 154
National Pensioners Convention, 166
National Transport Workers' Federation (NTWF), 26, 33, 35, 39
National Union of Agricultural and Allied Workers, 179-80
National Union of Agricultural Workers, 13
National Union of Dock Labourers, 22
National Union of Mineworkers, 8, 96, 174, 181
National Union of Vehicle Builders, 13, 67, 160, 202
National Union of Vehicle Workers, 39

New unionism, 23-4
Nicholas, Harry, 100, 111, 112, 114, 128, 131, 132
Nicholson, Brian, 176
Nuclear weapons, nuclear disarmament, 121-2, 123, 125, 127, 137, 176, 177, 212

O'Rourke, C., 60
Osborne judgement, 25

Papworth, Bert, 64, 65
Part, Ruby, 55
Part-time workers, 87, 149, 182, 183
Passenger transport industry, 35, 39, 41, 50, 51, 58, 62, 63, 69, 109, 115, 117; see also busworkers, cab drivers, tramwaymen
Passingham, Bernie, 143, 144, 146
Pay restraint, see incomes policy
Pemberton, Stan, 162, 202
Pentonville Five, 154-5, 156, 172
Phoenix Consortium, 199
Picketing, 154; secondary picketing, 156; mass picketing, 117, 161, 172
Plasterers Union, 159
Powell, Enoch, 150-2, 160
Pressed Steel Strike 1934, 67-8
Prosser, Margaret, 147, 149, 181, 183, 188, 201

Quaile, Mary, 68-9

Race equality, race equality legislation, 136, 149, 187-8, 211
Racism, 136, 149, 150, 152, 187
railway workers, railways, 22, 25, 26, 31, 35, 40, 58, 67
Rank-and-file workers, 64, 65, 68, 88, 115, 116, 134, 191
RMT, 40
Road haulage industry, road transport workers, 35, 39, 42, 62, 63, 99, 100, 102, 116, 117, 118, 159, 169, 175
Road Haulage Wages Act 1938, 63
Road Transport Act, 1930, 58
Roberts, Alf, 160
Robinson, Derek, 173

Rover, 174, 199-200
Ryde, George, 194

Sanders, Brenda, 184, 211
Sanders, George, 39
Scanlon, Hugh, 18, 137, 173, 198, 210
Scargill, Arthur, 175, 181
Scottish Commercial Motormen's Union, 159
Scottish Textile Workers, 120
Scottish Transport and General Workers Union, 62, 103, 160
Second World War, 77-9, 83-8
 – Bevin as Minister of Labour, 79-80
 – and women workers, 86-7
Shaw Inquiry 1920, 32-5
Shaw, Lord, 32, 33
shop stewards, 68, 85, 87, 100, 115, 141-2, 144, 205
Simpson, Derek, 19, 198, 201, 210, 212
Smith, Larry, 109
Snowden, Phillip, 58, 165
Social Contract, 162-5
Social Democratic Federation, 20
Social partnership, 54, 64, 184, 191, 196, 198, 202
Socialism, socialist values, 19-20, 22, 23, 24, 25, 26, 28, 30, 81, 91, 98, 121, 125, 141, 167, 208, 212, 215
South Side Labour Protection League, 22
Spanish civil war, 141, 157
Standard Motors, 120
Stevedores, Stevedores Union, 37, 40, 103, 110, 160, 181, 193
Strikes, 14, 15, 26, 27, 29, 31, 39, 40, 43, 48, 53, 54, 62, 64, 68, 69, 74, 84, 100, 102, 104-5, 107, 108, 117-8, 120, 133, 134, 140, 143, 144, 149, 150, 154, 156, 157, 162, 169, 173, 174; see also unofficial strikes
 – British Airways strike 1997, 193-4
 – Canadian Seamen's Union strike, 105
 – Coronation Strike, 64-5
 – Docks Strike 1889, 17-21
 – Docks Strike 1989, 184-5

– Ford sewing machinists strike, 146-7
– Gate Gourmet dispute, 206-8
– General Strike, 49-53, 56, 59, 79, 174
– Humber-Rootes strike, 100
– Liverpool docks strike 1995-8, 191, 193
– miners strike 1984, 174-5, 177, 184
– Pressed Steel Strike, 67-8

T&G Record, 51, 60, 69, 84, 128, 133, 154, 160, 174, 191
T&G Retired Members Association, 166
Taff Vale Judgement, 25
TASS, 140
Taylor, Harold, 89
Tewson, Vincent, 97
Textile industry, textile workers, 120, 152, 180, 181
Thatcher, Margaret, Thatcherism, 139, 151, 154, 165, 170, 171-2, 173, 174, 177, 179, 184, 185, 194, 198
Thomas, Jimmy, 58, 165
Thompson, Fred, 39
Thorne, Will, 15, 22
Tiffin, Arthur 'Jock', 111-2, 114, 116
Tillett, Ben, 17-18, 19-21, 22, 24, 26, 28, 34, 41, 47, 70
Tinplate industry, tinplate workers, 40, 62, 94
Todd, Ron, 97, 144, 176, 186, 187, 189, 214
– as General Secretary, 177-85
Tolpuddle Martyrs, 13, 179
Towers, John, 199
Trades Union Congress (TUC), 8, 14, 22, 23, 25, 54, 59, 65, 70, 82, 91, 96, 97, 99, 106, 110, 118, 123, 125, 127, 132, 134, 139, 149, 150,

154, 157, 163, 165, 173, 184, 196
– in general strike, 49-53
Tramwaymen, tramways, 48, 50, 51, 62
Transport House, 70, 109
Triple Alliance, 31
Turner, Vic, 155-6
Tyneside and National Labour Union, 22

Unifi, 209
Unilever, 100
Unite, 8, 18, 66, 298-214
United Road Transport Union, 39
United Vehicle Workers Union, 39
Unofficial strikes, unofficial action, 48, 64, 65, 71, 75, 100, 104, 105, 106, 107, 115, 121, 143
Upper Clyde Shipbuilders, 156
Urwin, Harry, 142

Varley, Julia, 56
Vauxhall, 143-4, 202

Wage restraint, *see* incomes policy
Webb, Beatrice, 19, 23, 31
Webb, Sydney, 19, 23, 31
Williams, Robert, 27
Williamson, Thomas, 97, 123, 125
Wilson, Harold, 98, 127, 128, 130, 131, 136, 137, 150, 154, 157, 163, 164, 173
'Winter of discontent' 1978-9, 169-70
Women in the union, 24, 39, 43, 55, 56, 67, 68-9, 86-7, 101, 102, 146-9, 163, 172, 181-4, 187, 210, 211
Woodley, Tony, 18, 143-4, 160, 178, 199-200
– as General Secretary, 201-15
Workers' Union, 55-7, 66
World Federation of Trade Unions, 108
Wright, George, 176, 187